MARTIAL ARTS SERIES

Judo
Techniques & Tactics

Jimmy Pedro
Fifth-Degree Black Belt
World Champion
Olympic Medalist

with

William Durbin
Third-Degree Black Belt

Human Kinetics

Library of Congress Cataloging-in-Publication Data

Pedro, Jimmy, 1970-
    Judo techniques & tactics / by Jimmy Pedro with William Durbin.
    p.   cm. -- (Martial arts series)
    Includes bibliographical references (p.) and index.
    ISBN 0-7360-0343-6
    1. Judo. I. Durbin, William, 1953- II. Title. III. Series.

    GV1114 .P43 2001
    796.815'2--dc21   00-054236

ISBN: 0-7360-0343-6
Copyright © 2001 by James Pedro

Writer: William Durbin; **Developmental Editor:** Cassandra Mitchell; **Assistant Editors:** Wendy McLaughlin, Dan Brachtesende; **Copyeditor:** Bob Replinger; **Proofreader:** Pam Johnson; **Indexer:** Betty Frizzell; **Permission Manager:** Toni Harte; **Graphic Designer:** Robert Reuther; **Graphic Artist:** Tara Welsch; **Photo Manager:** Clark Brooks; **Cover Designer:** Jack W. Davis; **Photographer (cover):** Bob Willingham; **Photographer (interior):** Tom Roberts; **Art Manager:** Craig Newsom; **Printer:** United Graphics

Human Kinetics books are available at special discounts for bulk purchase. Special editions or book excerpts can also be created to specification. For details, contact the Special Sales Manager at Human Kinetics.

Printed in the United States of America   10   9   8   7   6   5   4   3   2   1

Human Kinetics
Web site: http://www.humankinetics.com

United States: Human Kinetics, P.O. Box 5076, Champaign, IL 61825-5076
800-747-4457
e-mail: humank@hkusa.com

Canada: Human Kinetics, 475 Devonshire Road Unit 100, Windsor, ON N8Y 2L5
800-465-7301 (in Canada only)
e-mail: orders@hkcanada.com

Europe: Human Kinetics, Units C2/C3 Wira Business Park, West Park Ring Road,
Leeds LS16 6EB, United Kingdom
+44 (0)113 278 1708
e-mail: hk@hkeurope.com

Australia: Human Kinetics, 57A Price Avenue, Lower Mitcham, South Australia 5062
08 8277 1555
e-mail: liahka@senet.com.au

New Zealand: Human Kinetics, P.O. Box 105-231, Auckland Central
09-523-3462
e-mail: hkp@ihug.co.nz

CONTENTS

PREFACE

The Japanese martial art of judo is commonly assimilated with other martial arts such as karate, taekwondo, and kung fu. However, judo is vastly different from other martial arts in that no punches or kicks are allowed. Judo is more of a grappling martial art in which the object is to throw, pin, strangle, and even armlock your opponent into submission. Judo's main emphasis is on the ability to use your opponent's strength and momentum to your own advantage, thereby allowing you to defeat or overcome bigger and stronger adversaries. Judo is not only a physical battle, but also one of wits, whereby the successful judoka is able to anticipate an opponent's moves before they occur and react with one's own moves.

The study of judo offers benefits to all; people of any age or body type can practice it. Many people start as early as age 5 and some continue to practice the art through their 70s. For many people, judo provides a means to improve their general fitness level by increasing strength, flexibility, conditioning, coordination, and balance. For others, judo instills a sense of self-confidence, self-discipline, and self-control, all of which are necessary life skills. Parents like judo because it teaches their children discipline and respect. In addition to keeping its practitioners trim and fit, judo also provides people with invaluable self-defense skills.

For those who desire to compete, judo tournaments are held weekly at the local, regional, national, and international levels. Judo is a well-organized sport worldwide and is governed by one set of rules. There are no variations of judo, meaning that wherever you go to practice or compete in the sport, it is done the same way. Because of its worldwide popularity, judo was the first martial art accepted into the Olympic Games (Tokyo, 1964). Currently, there are approximately 175 nations that compete in the sport, making it the second-most contested sport in the modern Olympic Games.

Judo Techniques & Tactics was written and designed to benefit judo practitioners of all levels. It covers a wide variety of topics from history and philosophy to the rules and terminology, and it offers training and competition tips as well. For the beginner, this book describes judo's history, philosophy, and basic concepts, and it provides step-by-step instruction of each technique for easy understanding. The intermediate judoka will benefit from the book's explanation of tactics, competition rules, and conditioning and training methods used by successful judo players. A greater understanding of the techniques and concepts will further enhance the intermediate judoka's knowledge and skills to become a better judoka. The advanced judoka will find the chapters on training and conditioning the most interesting and beneficial and may use the technique chapters as a reference to help clarify the basics.

Chapter 1 begins by familiarizing you with the value of judo and provides some criteria for selecting a good school and instructor. Chapter 2 provides an overview of the history and philosophy of judo. Chapter 3 covers the terminology, derived from its Japanese roots, used in most judo training.

Chapters 4 through 9 contain illustrated, step-by-step descriptions of the various judo techniques. Falls and rolls are covered in chapter 4. Chapter 5 addresses the basic stances and grips of judo. In Chapter 6 you will begin to learn the really fun part of judo: throwing. This chapter covers the basic elements of a throw and describes how to perform the most popular judo throws used in competition today. Chapter 7 contains descriptions and illustrations of all of the basic pins and hold-downs. In Chapter 8 you will find a wide variety of chokes and arm locks. Chapter 9 shows how to put some of these techniques together in combinations to create effective judo. In chapter 10 you will learn the rules of judo competition. Finally, chapter 11 covers flexibility, strength, and endurance exercises to improve your judo performance.

Judo Techniques & Tactics will prove to be a valuable tool if you keep the following guidelines in mind. Be sure to select the techniques that work best for your body type. Read the technique descriptions carefully and follow the step-by-step instructions. Learn one technique at a time and try to perfect it before moving on to others. It is better to master one technique that will work against every opponent than to be familiar with a dozen that only work against weak opponents. Be patient. Judo techniques require a lot of effort and practice and cannot be learned overnight. Don't do too much too soon. It is better to work out for short periods of time three times per week and build stamina than get burned out by practicing two hours every day.

Although this book places a lot of emphasis on the skills, tactics, and techniques of judo competitors, it is not necessary to participate in competition to enjoy judo or get value from this book. The majority of judo players do not actually compete, but are more recreational judoka who enjoy the benefits of practicing judo. Judo can be a fun, challenging, and exciting sport for anyone interested in getting in shape, learning self-defense, and competing whether it be in the dojo or at the international level. The techniques and concepts provided in this book will make your judo experience a most enjoyable one regardless of what your aspirations may be.

ACKNOWLEDGMENTS

Throughout my career I was fortunate that so many different people genuinely cared about my success and development as an athlete and as an individual. Although I cannot thank everyone individually, I would like to express my thanks and gratitude to those around me for their help and assistance. Without your support, devotion, love, friendship, and generosity I would never have attained the level of success I've enjoyed throughout my judo career.

I would like to take this opportunity to thank the following people:

My father, Jim, has always been there as my coach and best friend. He provided me with a solid foundation in judo, which has given me direction and been the key to my success. Perhaps most importantly, he instilled the discipline and positive work ethic that inspired me to be an Olympian.

My mother, Susanne, has always provided me with emotional support when I needed it most. Her comfort, love, and support helped me get through the most difficult of times.

Marie, my wife, has always supported me and allowed me to pursue my dreams. Thank you for your understanding, love, and the countless sacrifices you have made.

My children, Casey, A.J., and Ricky, have provided me with the motivation to succeed.

I thank my sister, Tanya, and brother, Mike for their love and support. Thanks for the memories, tears, and joy we shared.

I thank my in-laws, Richard and Suzuko, for taking care of my wife and children while I was frequently on the road.

My friend and teammate, Jason Morris, helped me believe I could succeed and shared many years of memories and friendship.

My Olympic coach and friend, Steve Cohen, made many sacrifices to ensure that I had everything I needed to be my best each day.

My strength and conditioning coach, Paul Soucy, made sure I was always the best-conditioned athlete on the mat.

I would also like to thank Neil Adams, Nittai University, Nichidai University, Keischo, and many others for allowing me to train at their dojo.

USA Judo and the New York Athletic Club believed in me and provided financial support throughout my career.

Alex and Diana Kiesel at Yang's Martial Arts allowed me to pass my knowledge on to my students at Pedro's Judo Club, and my students have made teaching fun!

Lastly, thanks to all of the people who treated me like one of their own family members and allowed me to stay with them while I trained. I thank the Sunadas in Hawaii, the Hommas in Japan, the Kneitingers in Germany, and the Westwoods in England for their hospitality and generosity.

CHAPTER

1

GETTING
STARTED

J udo is a sport with its origins in the martial art of jujutsu. Sometime in the 16th century, the term *jujutsu* was coined as the generic term for empty-hand martial arts in Japan. Before its acceptance as an Olympic sport in 1964, judo was a system of self-defense founded by Jigoro Kano.

Judo has its roots in the ancient samurai empty-hand martial art, which was based on grappling. Many names were originally applied to the empty-hand arts in Japan, among them *torite, wajutsu, yawara, kogusoku, taijutsu,* and *kempo.*

In 1882 a young master by the name of Jigoro Kano started his own school, which he called the *Kodokan.* Kano chose to refer to his art as *judo.* Just as jujutsu meant "gentle art," judo means "gentle way." Kano preferred this term because he wanted his students not only to develop excellent martial arts skill but also to learn how to live a gentle life.

The object of the sport of judo is to throw, pin, choke, or joint lock your opponent into submission. There are no strikes, punches, or kicks, differentiating it from many other martial arts. Even when learning judo as self-defense, *judoka* (judo pupils), learn how to defend punches, kicks, and weapons with throws, chokes, and joint locks. Judo is an excellent method of self-defense when taught appropriately.

The greatest value of judo lies in its emphasis on gentleness as a lifestyle. Judo teaches the person to avoid conflict and seek gentle resolutions to all conflict. Jigoro Kano taught that judoka should live by the principle of mutual benefit to all. This meant that although the judoka took care of themselves, they were also concerned about other people, including opponents.

This principle also affects the concept of training. In many other martial arts, a practitioner cares only about developing personal skill, but the judoka tries to help everyone in the *dojo* (school) improve. This aspect is a main tenet of judo as developed by its founder. All judo dojo stress mutual benefit.

Another benefit of judo training is that the practitioner learns to practice the second principle that Jigoro Kano emphasized—achieving maximum efficiency with minimum effort. In life we can accomplish any task in two ways—the hard way and the efficient way. Through judo training a practitioner learns to use the body efficiently. He or she learns how to use the least amount of strength to accomplish the technical goal, be it throwing, locking, or choking. Yet the physical aspect is only part of the principle. A person learns that every problem can be solved efficiently, without depleting one's resources.

Judo is a gentle way of life that teaches people to live fully, seeking benefit for all people while achieving the most they can from their talents. A judoka seeks to benefit his or her life while helping others as well. Most of all, a judoka becomes a credit to society by following the principles laid down by Jigoro Kano in the establishment of the philosophy of judo.

BENEFITS OF JUDO

When Kano founded judo, he wanted it to be a method that would benefit the lives of judo practitioners in every way. First, judo is an excellent form of physical fitness. Through the *taiso,* or exercises, a person builds the body in both strength and flexibility. Through the practice of the skills of judo, the body becomes stronger and cardiovascular endurance develops.

The judo practitioner can focus the mind more sharply and attain a higher level of concentration. These capabilities benefit not only the practice of judo but also the scholastic capability of the student or the efficiency of the adult on the job. Through the mental training of judo, the practitioner learns how to keep calm under pressure, a facility that affects everything from driving to test taking to the normal pressures of raising a family and earning a living.

The mental training of judo also teaches flexibility of mind, which allows the judoka to be more open-minded and capable of being spontaneous in all aspects of life. This attribute is especially valuable for the calmness it produces, which helps to lower blood pressure and avoid the stress of hypertension.

When a person truly begins to follow the discipline of judo as a way of life, he or she will generally practice daily. This schedule leads to a dedicated manner of living so that all aspects of the person's life receive the benefits of that discipline. Students study more efficiently, workers perform their jobs with greater dedication, and all aspects of life take on greater order. The judoka realizes that everything has an order and a purpose and that skills can be used most efficiently when used appropriately.

All this leads to greater self-confidence. When students begin to feel good about themselves, they begin to have confidence to engage in other challenges. Through the practice of judo, many shy people find the strength to get out and meet people, set goals, and achieve great things.

One final benefit that one can gain through judo is the ability to defend oneself. It must be noted that judo needs to be taught as a form of self-defense for this goal to be achieved. Many excellent judo instructors still emphasize this aspect of judo. Judo taught as a form of self-defense seeks to make small persons capable of defending themselves against much larger and stronger opponents. Although the program of judo will make a person stronger, it is always acknowledged that attackers prey on the weak. When a person is obviously strong, few people will view that person as prey. But on those occasions when a larger, violent person attacks, the skills of judo, based on "yielding" to the assault, allow the practitioner to turn the assailant's strength against that person.

Judo as a form of self-defense teaches a full range of punches, strikes, kicks, and blocking techniques. These skills are not allowed in the sport of judo, but one must learn them for real self-defense skill. Another aspect of judo as a form of self-defense is the use of holds and joint locks that are illegal in the sport. Self-defense judo uses methods of attacking and joint twisting that cannot be allowed in sport because of the incredible damage that such moves would inflict if carried to their conclusion. This kind of result, however, is sometimes necessary in self-defense.

The benefits of judo are endless. The longer one trains, the more benefits the person sees. Judo affects all aspects of one's life, including longevity. Because of the health benefits of judo, many of the masters of judo lived longer, more active lives than those around them. Taught and practiced properly, judo is a lifetime activity of great benefit to its practitioners.

SELECTING A JUDO SCHOOL

When picking a martial arts school, or dojo, one should know what he or she wants and then choose the school accordingly. Because it is the "gentle" way, judo appeals to many people. Yet one must understand that "gentle" is a relative term and that judo, especially when practiced competitively, can be rough and rugged.

The person who wants to participate in judo as a sport should be prepared for hard workouts and strenuous training, which will be rewarding in competition. State, national, and international competitions are available to the student desiring to compete.

When choosing a school in which to train in judo as a sport, one should be sure that the teacher has experience in the competitive arena. Many excellent instructors in today's judo dojo were past competitors or are even current competitors.

Only someone who has been on the mat in national and international competition will be able to understand all aspects of judo competition. Those who set the Olympics as their goal will need to understand the nuances of international competition. An experienced coach is necessary to compete in the international arena.

The other side of judo is self-defense. When first introduced outside Japan, judo was presented as a method of self-defense. Like competitive judo, self-defense judo has unique aspects. A great competitor does not always understand self-defense, just as a great self-defense master does not fully understand competition. Therefore, if a person wants to learn judo as a method of self-defense, he or she should seek a person with self-defense experience or a person who has been trained by a combat judo instructor. Many excellent combat judo masters have been trained in the military or have been police officers of some type. Some of the best judo masters in the world have extensive street expertise through military or law-enforcement experience.

Most self-defense judo training is more moderate than competitive training, emphasizing skill rather than endurance and strength. Self-defense judo tries to build up a person's endurance and strength gradually, with a realistic goal of working daily training into a person's life. Thus, the emphasis is on developing skill that can offset an attacker's strength and size. On the other hand, like any sport, competitive judo relies on the development of endurance, strength, and skill so that one can compete against other well-trained judoka.

Thus, when choosing a judo school, one should begin by asking himself or herself these questions: "What do I want to learn? Do I want to compete? Do I want to learn self-defense?" Once these questions have been answered, one should check the qualifications of the instructor to be sure that the instructor has the right type of training, either competitive or self-defense.

When checking out an instructor, one should ask to see credentials. Many have their qualifications on the walls of their dojo, and all legitimate instructors will show their certificates to a prospective student. If a person has any doubt, he or she can contact the appropriate martial-arts organization to verify a person's rank, training, and current standing. One should be wary of people who tell elaborate stories about why they are no longer part of their organization. Rarely are people expelled without good reason. Those who leave an organization will generally join another if they are legitimate judoka.

The prospective student should watch a class before joining a dojo. Instructors have different personalities. The student should pick an instructor who teaches the desired type of judo, and the instructor should be one to whom the student can relate. The student need not personally "like" the instructor, but the student should feel comfortable with the instructor, feel capable of following the teacher's instructions, and be confident in the instructor's ability. Some instructors are militaristic, whereas others prefer a family type of atmosphere in the dojo. The student should be sure that the atmosphere of the dojo is one that he or she can enjoy and learn in.

Dojo take many different forms. Some are located in storefronts. Others are in YMCA or college facilities. A few instructors have built their own buildings. For judo, mat space is a necessity. Judo cannot be taught without the safety of mats, and one should hesitate to train with a judo instructor who does not have mats.

Methods of payments vary, as do costs, according to the cost of living in the particular area. Some schools charge as little as $30 a month, whereas others charge as much as $150. One should be wary of contracts that require a commitment to paying for a year of lessons or ask for too much money in a lump sum. In addition, one should never train at a school that guarantees a black belt in a certain time. A black belt is earned through hard work, training, and meeting qualifications. It is impossible to set a specific schedule for any student, and to do so is fraudulent. Some students have earned black belts in 3 years. Others have taken 10. To reach a goal, the student must be dedicated and must put in the time and effort. No instructor can guarantee that a student will be motivated.

BELT RANKING SYSTEM

Jigoro Kano created the belt system to modernize his school along Western lines, just as the rest of Japan was seeking modernization during the Meiji Restoration. Kano broke the ranks into two levels—kyu and dan. *Kyu,* usually translated as "class," refers to preliminary training or preparatory education. People who hold kyu ranks are known as *mudansha,* literally meaning "person without degree."

Dan, usually translated as "degree," is likened to degrees of education. In the same way that schools have 12 grades, so too did Jigoro Kano establish 12 degrees. Kano never awarded a degree higher than 10th degree. Thus 10th degree is usually the highest rank awarded in judo and most legitimate martial arts. People who hold dan degrees are known as *yudansha,* literally "person with a degree."

Kyu ranks, when originally created by Kano, were symbolized by a white belt, and the dan ranks wore black belts. Eventually Kano added a brown belt for the highest levels of kyu, a red and white belt for master ranks, and finally the solid red belt for senior master ranks (see table 1.1).

In modern times other colors have been added to the kyu levels, with variations appearing in different countries. Beginners always start with a white belt, but some judo schools then use yellow, green, purple, blue, or other colors for belts of the other kyu levels.

People in the first five dan ranks usually wear solid black belts, and those in the 6th through 8th ranks wear a red and white section belt. Finally, those who have earned the 9th or 10th degree wear a solid red belt. People who have earned a 5th-degree black belt or above are known by a special term—*kodansha.*

TABLE 1.1
Kodokan Judo Ranking System

Name	Level	Belt
Rokkyu	Sixth-class kyu	White
Gokyu	Fifth-class kyu	White
Yonkyu	Fourth-class kyu	White
Sankyu	Third-class kyu	Brown
Nikkyu	Second-class kyu	Brown
Ikkyu	First-class kyu	Brown
Shodan	First-degree dan	Black
Nidan	Second-degree dan	Black
Sandan	Third-degree dan	Black
Yodan	Fourth-degree dan	Black
Godan	Fifth-degree dan	Black
Rokudan	Sixth-degree dan	Black or red & white
Shichidan	Seventh-degree dan	Black or red & white
Hachidan	Eighth-degree dan	Black or red & white
Kudan	Ninth-degree dan	Black or solid red
Judan	Tenth-degree dan	Black or solid red

When judo first entered the United States and as it spread around the world, the idea of earning a black belt became a wondrous goal. For many people, the black belt symbolized absolute mastery of combat skill. Most believed that a person with a black belt was undefeatable. In Japan, however, this is not the attitude.

A black belt is a symbol of knowledge, of learning, similar to a diploma. *Shodan,* the first-degree black belt, translates as "beginner." Therefore, a person who has earned a black belt has finally learned enough to become a serious student. The goal of training is to develop the discipline to engage in judo practice on a daily basis. The black belt is a symbol of discipline and hard work.

A person who holds the black belt has the responsibility of acting with the image of a true judoka—of being a gentle person and living a life of peace and harmony with others. A black belt is a symbol of mature development through the avenue of judo.

EQUIPMENT

When judo was first introduced to the West, it was said that no special equipment was needed to engage in training. Although this is true of the self-defense *kata,* part of the curriculum of judo, it is not necessarily true for competition judo.

Absolutely essential to judo training is a good set of mats. They must have thickness sufficient to ensure the safety of judo students when they take throws. All judo skills can be developed and practiced on mats. People must never wear shoes on the mats because the soles of shoes may pick up small rocks and other items. When a person walks across a mat with shoes on, those items can become stuck to the mat, where they can damage the feet and bodies of people practicing judo.

The next necessity for judo training is a *judo gi,* the proper uniform. This costume gives the students a uniformity of purpose and a sense of belonging. Many different types of practice uniforms (often called *keikogi)* are worn, but the judogi is a uniform designed especially for the grappling training of judo. The top, the *uwagi,* or jacket, is a single- or double-weave cotton uniform, heavy enough that it will not tear when a partner pulls on it. The *zubon* are the pants of judo, usually of strong construction, with an extra patch of material at the knees.

Finally, the judoka crosses the uniform top left over right and uses an *obi,* or belt, to hold the top together. As stated previously, the color of the belt denotes rank. The obi is a piece of cotton, folded multiple times to make a strong belt, not easily torn or damaged.

Access to a weight set or machine is considered essential to modern judo training. For competition, the benefit of strength cannot be overemphasized. Although excellent skill is indispensable, in competition against a skilled opponent, well-developed strength can mean the difference between success and failure.

A judo gi, the proper judo uniform.

Strength training will be discussed further in chapter 11. But keep in mind that developing the skills of judo requires only a mat, a uniform, and a good training partner.

Judo is both an excellent form of physical training and a way to develop the mind of the practitioner. Judo has solid philosophical grounding in the principles of Jigoro Kano. These principles are designed to make the judoka a better person and, through his or her actions, make the world a better place. For those wishing some form of competition, judo is an excellent sport. When taught with the proper emphasis, judo can also be an effective means of self-defense. Whether as a sport or a self-defense art, judo promotes physical fitness, longevity, and self-confidence.

CHAPTER

2

ROOTS OF
JUDO

This chapter gives a general history of judo from its origins of Kodokan judo, to its development as a philosophical doctrine, to the current standing of judo competition in the United States and at the international level.

ORIGINS OF JUDO

The history of modern judo begins with the great martial-arts master, Jigoro Kano. Born the third son of Jirosaku Mareshiba Kano and his wife Sadako on October 28, 1860, Jigoro Kano grew up in a changing Japan. The Meiji Restoration began in 1868, and Japan raced to become a nation that could match the power of any Western country.

Kano was educated in Tokyo at the private schools of Seitatsu Shojuku and Ikuei Gijuku. At the latter school he studied English and German. His education took him to the Tokyo School of Foreign Languages, Kaisei School, and eventually to the Tokyo

Imperial University, from which he graduated in 1881, majoring in literature, politics, and political economy.

Kano was first introduced to jujutsu when, at age 18, he enrolled in the Tenshin Shinyo Ryu jujutsu dojo of Hachinosuke Fukuda. During this time more than 700 different systems of jujitsu existed and over the next few years Kano studied as many different forms as he could. He saw that by combining the best techniques of various schools into one system, he could create a physical education system that would embody mental and physical skill. He also believed these techniques could be practiced as a competitive sport.

In 1882 at age 22, Kano opened the first Kodokan judo dojo, teaching at the Eishoji Buddhist temple. He decided to use the term *judo* rather than the word *jujutsu* for philosophical reasons, emphasizing the doctrine of gentleness as a way of living rather than only the principle of yielding as a fighting concept. Too many jujutsu practitioners at the time had bad reputations and lived the lives of ruffians. Jigoro Kano wanted to make his art appealing to people of all walks of life and create a situation in which the art would have a profound influence on his students, making them genuinely gentle people. Thus he emphasized the concept of judo, living a "gentle way."

Thus in its beginnings, the Kodokan was a school of Kito Ryu jujutsu, with an emphasis on the philosophical meaning of *ju*. In the sense of physical skills, ju can refer to yielding, that is, giving way to an attacker's force in order to use it against the attacker or dissipate it so that it cannot cause hurt. Kano discovered that a throw was only as successful as the breaking of the balance of the opponent. The effectiveness of the throw was thus dependent on taking the person off balance. The practitioner accomplished this through the process of yielding, the application of ju. From a philosophical point of view, ju refers to being gentle and flexible in thought. Thus Kano was hoping to teach his students to be better people by being gentle individuals. The principle of ju was thus defined as "push when pulled and pull when pushed."

At this point Kano had a small body of students who trained hard and sought to build and develop the system for their master. As the years passed, the reputation of the Kodokan grew. Kano created a method of *randori* (sparring) that excluded striking and dangerous techniques and allowed "friendly" competition with other jujutsu schools. Generally, the great throwing skills of the Kodokan, based on those of the Kito Ryu and further developed by the research of Kano himself, were sufficient to defeat all comers.

Another of the greatest judo students at the Kodokan was Shiro Saigo, who was a trained exponent of *oshikiuchi,* a style of the Takeda family that would eventually be called Daito Ryu Aikijujutsu. Saigo faced many opponents of the Kodokan, beating them handily with his knowledge and advanced Kodokan training.

An event in 1886 helped strengthen the reputation of the Kodokan. Although free exchange had occurred between the Kodokan and some jujutsu schools, other schools were extremely jealous of the growth of the new school. Some of these schools formed an organization with the idea of resisting the growth of the Kodokan.

A competition was held to determine the superior art. Each dojo was allowed 15 competitors. Kano's students won 13 of the matches, with the other 2 being draws. This event launched the Kodokan as a preeminent school of martial arts in Japan.

Kano himself attained the degree of the 12th dan and is the only judoka to ever have received this level. A high-ranking judoka once said that randori with the master, Jigoro Kano, was like fighting an empty jacket.

Kano's life from that time on was one of travel, work in the field of education, and teaching Kodokan judo. In 1909 Kano became the first Japanese member of the International Olympic Committee. In 1922 he was elected to the House of Peers, and in 1928 he attended the Olympic Games in Amsterdam as a member of the International Olympic Committee.

Kano believed in the "way of gentleness" and mastered it as a principle of both life and martial arts. He loved life and believed that people should strive constantly to improve themselves, an idea he tried to encourage through his judo teachings.

Jigoro Kano also believed in education. Whether it was schooling in martial arts, in liberal arts, or in higher education, Kano encouraged everyone to develop a zeal for life and a joy in progress. He lived his life with the idea that a person could make a difference not only during his or her lifetime but also in the generations to come.

Kano believed that a virtuous person could make the world a better place. He proved that idea by doing so himself. More than

60 years after his death on May 4, 1938, Kano continues to exert a positive influence on judo practitioners and all martial artists. Kano, who could be called the gentle master, lived his life following his judo, his "way of gentleness."

THE DEVELOPMENT OF JUDO AS A PHILOSOPHICAL DOCTRINE

Jigoro Kano was both an educator and a philosopher. He did not advocate a specific religious philosophy, however, because he wanted to teach a way of life that anyone who practiced his martial art could accept. Thus his philosophy was that of judo, a philosophy that he believed people of any country and any faith could abide by.

When Jigoro Kano began the study of jujutsu, he saw in it more than just a method of fighting. First, he realized that if his country were to prosper, the people needed to be physically fit. Jujutsu training could accomplish that goal.

Next, he realized that the people needed to develop themselves mentally, not only by accumulating knowledge but also by developing a strength and creativity of mind that would allow them to adapt to a changing world.

Finally, he saw a need for moral development. The Japanese, who tended toward ritualistic beliefs and the performance of sacraments but did not necessarily concern themselves with moral rectitude, needed a unified method of moral development. During this time of transformation in Japan, some people, especially the young, found in the loss of cultural stability a void into which they sank without a source of moral guidance. Bands of roving *soshi,* delinquents, preyed on the weak. Kano hoped that his judo would be capable of either changing them or giving innocent people the skill to deal with them. Either way, Kano hoped to fill the void left by the dissolution of the feudal era and the uncertainty of the Meiji Restoration.

Kano hoped to fill the emptiness by introducing judo, not as a fighting art or martial sport but as a way of life. The first goal of judo was to give each practitioner a gentle outlook on life. Although judo training could release the energy and stress of youth and life in a positive manner, it could also develop calmness that permitted a judoka to remain composed and peaceful in everyday life. A person can perform better in any life situation if he or she can remain tranquil.

These three ideas of Kodokan judo—rentai ho, shobu ho, and shushin ho—are the foundation on which individual cultivation is based. By practicing these three methods, one learns the two main principles of Kodokan judo.

Beginning with *rentai ho,* Kano wanted judo to train the entire body. He felt that most sports neglected the muscles not necessary to the specific activity. Judo methodically trained all the muscles of the human body. *Nage no kata,* the form of throwing, was developed to practice throws on both sides, thus balancing the improvement of the muscles. Randori allowed free training of the movements of the body and developed the mind as well

The practice of both *kata* and randori was intended to be based on the principle of *seiryoku zenyo,* which is maximum, efficient use of power. This was the concept of ju—reliance not on sheer physical strength but on efficient use of what strength one had.

Shobu ho, the use of judo as a sport, was for limited use. Kano originally thought that the sport form would bring young people into the practice of the martial arts. The idea was for people to practice randori to develop certain skills, both mental and physical. Young people could then periodically test their mettle in friendly competition. To keep the event on a friendly basis, lethal techniques and those that would cause serious injury were not permitted. To promote safety, students were instructed to surrender to the throw or capitulate to the choke or joint lock.

The emphasis in *shiai,* competitive matches, was on good technique, rhythm, timing, and the other elements of movement as well as the development of the concept of ju through the perfection of the principle of seiryoku zenyo.

Kano was concerned that competition would become too important, so he continually emphasized that shiai was designed to bring young people into the art. In contrast, people of all ages could practice kata, an activity that could last a lifetime. Kano's desire was for Kodokan judo to create an interest in the martial arts. As a person aged, he or she would continue to practice the ancient martial arts that Kano was preserving in the Kodokan Kobudo Kenkyu Kai.

Finally, there was *shushin ho,* which was judo as an ethical and moral discipline based on the principle of *jita kyoei*, or mutual prosperity and cooperation. To Kano, judo was a true way of life. To live with the genuine principle of ju was to live a life that brought benefit not only to oneself but also to others.

Kano's judo was a way of training in the dojo so that everyone benefited. Each student was expected to care about the other students. The goal of training together was for each person to benefit from the knowledge and skill of the others. The spontaneity and creativity developed during randori practice were intended to be applicable in everyday life.

Kodokan judo skills and development produced a strong, confident, focused, aware, and decisive person—a person who would benefit society by living with good manners and moral standards. The judoka as a member of society would be flexible, yet firmly grounded. In essence, judo creates a person who contributes to society.

This, then, is Kodokan judo as created by Jigoro Kano. More than just another physical activity, it emphasizes moral and spiritual training as well as physical training. The ultimate goal of judo is to perfect the individual so he or she can be valuable to society.

JUDO IN THE UNITED STATES AND AROUND THE WORLD

The United States had its first introduction to judo in the late 1800s. Beginning in 1889, Kano traveled abroad to Europe and the United States eight times to teach judo. Several of Kano's students devoted their lives to developing judo in foreign countries.

In 1904 Yoshiaki Yamashita, one of Kano's students, traveled to the United States and taught judo to President Theodore Roosevelt at a personal dojo in the White House. Yamashita continued to teach in the United States until 1907, when he returned to the Kodokan in Japan.

During the 1930s judo was taught at several colleges in California. In 1932 Kano lectured on judo at the University of Southern California. In that same year four American associations were formed and later became recognized by the Kodokan as representatives of American judo.

In 1962 the International Judo Federation was formed and became the governing body for judo internationally. In the United States, United States Judo Inc. became the governing body for judo along with the member organizations USJA (United States Judo Association) and USJF (United States Judo Federation).

Judo was first introduced into the Olympics in 1964 when they were held in Tokyo, Japan. In that year there were 74 participants from 27 different countries. By 1992 the competition had grown to 437 participants from 93 countries. In 1992 judo for women was added to the Olympics as an official medal sport.

About 7,000 people in the United States are currently members of the national organization USA Judo, and about 20,000 people are a member of one of the three national organizations of judo (United States Judo Inc., USJA, USJF). Judo is practiced by millions of men, women, and children all over the world.

Since its origin, judo has changed and grown as a discipline. Today it appeals to a wide variety of people. In the next chapter you'll learn more about the language and customs of judo as you become part of the growing judo community.

CHAPTER

3

LANGUAGE AND CUSTOMS OF JUDO

The terminology of judo is based on the Japanese language simply because Japan is the land of its origin. It is important to learn the names of all the techniques in Japanese for a number of reasons. The first purpose of learning Japanese terms is so that people from all countries, with varying languages, can communicate and compete in this international art with a common terminology.

Whether a person is in England, Germany, or Japan, an *ogoshi* is a hip throw. The common vocabulary makes it convenient for people to work together on the art of judo, even when they do not speak the same language. By using the Japanese term itself, students from all countries can understand what others are saying. Therefore, no matter where you go in the world to study judo, by knowing the terminology you will understand what the instructor, your training partner, and everybody else is referring to.

Second, it is imperative to learn the Japanese terminology associated with competition so that you will understand the commands made by the referee. During competitions all scoring and commands are usually given in Japanese. There are many a judoka who have lost a competition they should have won because they didn't understand what the referee was saying.

Third, it is easier for everybody to refer to a technique by using one word rather than trying to translate it into your own language. For example, it is easier for a coach to say "seionage" during a match than to tell you to do the two-handed shoulder throw.

One last aspect of learning Japanese terminology is respect. The founder of judo was Japanese. Using the Japanese language is a sign of respect for the country of origin, the founder, and the original masters of the art. Because judo and all martial arts center on courtesy, which by Japanese standards involves showing respect in the proper way, judo students must learn Japanese terminology.

COMMON TERMINOLOGY

The following are the most common terms used in judo, with which all practitioners and competitors of judo should be familiar. Pronunciation guidelines are included to help you learn the correct Japanese pronunciation

THE COMMONLY USED TERMS OF JUDO

Japanese	English
Judo jutsugo (ju-sue-go)	Terminology of judo
Anza (an-za)	Informal sitting, cross-legged
Ashi waza (ah-she-wah-zah)	Leg techniques
Awase waza (ah-wah-say-wah-zah)	Winning through the use of two incomplete techniques
Ayumi ashi (ah-yu-me-ah-she)	Normal walking
Dan (dahn)	Degrees of black belts

Japanese	English
Dojo (doh-jo)	School or training hall; literally, the place of the way
Fusegi (foo-say-gee)	Defenses against techniques
Goshinho (go-shin-hoh)	Methods of self-defense
Goshinjutsu (go-shin-jut-soo)	Art of self-defense
Hansoku make (han-so-koo-mah-kay)	Violation of rules in competition
Hantei (han-tay)	Verbal designation of the winner in a competition, given by the referee
Henka (hen-kah)	A variation on a technique
Hikiwake (he-ke-wah-kay)	A draw in a competition
Ippon shobu (e-pon-sho-boo)	A competition decided by one point
Itami wake (e-ta-me-wah-kay)	A loss in a competition caused by an injury and inability to continue
Jigo hontai (gee-goh-hon-tie)	Defensive basic posture
Jikan (gee-kan)	Time out command by a referee
Joseki (jo-say-kee)	The upper seat in a dojo for senior judoka
Judo gi (joo-doh-gee)	Practice uniform specifically designed for judo, extra heavy weight and double weave
Junbi undo (joon-bee-oon-doh)	Warm-up exercises
Kaeshi waza (kah-a-she-wah-zah)	Countering techniques
Kake (kah-kay)	The actual execution of a throw; literally, attack
Kamiza (kah-me-zah)	Upper seat, the place where the instructor stands at the beginning of class, also the place where the picture of Kano or other dignitaries hang
Kansetsu waza (kan-say-soo-wah-zah)	Joint-locking techniques
Kata (kah-tah)	Prearranged form of techniques, ceremonial in judo

Japanese	English
Katame waza (kah-tah-may-wah-zah)	Grappling techniques
Kega (kay-gah)	Injury
Keiko (kay-ko)	Practice
Keikogi (kay-ko-gee)	Practice uniform
Kiai (key-eye)	Spirit yell, a shout given at the point of technical execution
Kodansha (koh-don-sha)	High-ranking black belt, usually fifth-degree black belt and above
Kohai (ko-hi)	Junior, a person of a lower rank
Koshi waza (koh-she-wah-zah)	Hip techniques
Kumi kata (koo-me-kah-tah)	Forms of gripping
Kuzushi (coo-zoo-she)	Breaking balance before throwing; literally, destroy
Kyu (koo)	Class of rank below black belt
Maitta (ma-e-tah)	Verbal acknowledgment of defeat
Mate (mah-tay)	Command used by the referee to wait, permitting no further action in a competition
Mo sukoshi (moh-sue-koh-she)	Referee command meaning a little more is needed to score
Mudansha (moo-dahn-sha)	Person who does not hold a black belt
Nage waza (nah-gay-wah-zah)	Throwing techniques
Ne waza (nay-wah-zah)	Lying techniques
Nogare kata (noh-gah-ray-kah-tah)	Forms of escape
Obi (oh-bee)	Belt used to hold the uniform together; color of belt designates rank
Osaekomi (oh-say-koh-me)	Term used by the referee to indicate a pin is in effect in a competition
Osaekomi toketa (oh-say-koh-me-toh-kay-tah)	Term used by the referee to note that a pin has been broken

Japanese	English
Osaekomi waza (oh-say-koh-me-wah-zah)	Pinning techniques
Randori (ron-doh-ree)	Free play or sparring
Rei (ray)	Bow
Reigisaho (ray-gee-sah-hoh)	Mat etiquette
Reishiki (ray-she-key)	Japanese etiquette
Renraku waza (ren-rah-koo-wah-zah)	Connecting, combination techniques
Renshu (ren-shoo)	Training
Renzoku waza (ren-zoh-koo-wah-zah)	Continuous techniques of the same skill
Ritsurei (ree-soo-ray)	Standing bow
Ryu (roo)	School or system of martial art
Seiza (say-zah)	Formal Japanese way of sitting on the knees, with the buttocks on the heels
Sempai (sem-pie)	Senior, a person of a higher rank
Shiai (she-eye)	Competition
Shime waza (she-may-wah-zah)	Choking techniques
Shimoseki (she-moh-say-key)	Lower seat, the side the students line up on
Shintai (shin-tie)	Advancing and retreating movements
Shizen hontai (she-zen-hon-tie)	Natural basic posture
Shumatsu undo (shoo-mah-soo-oon-doh)	Cool-down exercises
Sotai renshu (soh-tie-ren-shoo)	Partner practice
Tachi waza (tah-chee-wah-zah)	Standing techniques
Taisabaki (tie-sah-bah-key)	Body movements
Taiso (tie-soh)	General term for exercises
Tandoku renshu (ton-doh-koo-ren-shoo)	Solo practice
Tatami (ta-ta-me)	Mats on which the martial arts are practiced

Japanese	English
Te waza (tay-wah-zah)	Hand techniques
Tokui waza (toh-koo-e-wah-zah)	Favorite technique, one's forte
Tori (to-ree)	Taker, the person performing the technique
Tsugi ashi (sue-gee-ah-she)	Following foot, shuffle
Tsukuri (sue-coo-ree)	Positioning for the throw; literally, build
Tsurikomi (sue-ree-koh-me)	Lift pull
Uchikomi (oo-che-koh-me)	Fitting in throwing practice without actually throwing
Uke (oo-kay)	Receiver, the person receiving the technique
Ukemi (oo-kay-mee)	Methods of falling safely
Uwagi (oo-wah-gee)	Jacket of the practice uniform
Waza (wah-zah)	Techniques
Waza ari (wah-za-a-ree)	Command used by the referee to award a half point
Waza ari awasete ippon (wah-za-a-ree-ah-wah-say-tay-e-pon)	One point earned by two half points
Yudansha (yoo-don-sha)	Person who holds a black belt
Yuseigachi (yoo-say-gah-chee)	Command used by the referee to award a victory by superiority
Zanshin (zan-shin)	Aware and alert mind over a controlled or defeated competitor
Zarei (zah-ray)	Kneeling bow
Zazen (zah-zen)	Kneeling meditation to compose and center oneself before competition
Zubon (zoo-bon)	Pants of the practice uniform

DOJO PROTOCOL

An ancient saying goes, "Martial arts practice begins and ends with courtesy." This idea, known as *reishiki,* is an important part of any true martial-arts training. Dojo around the world have different levels of emphasis in reishiki, but typical judo dojo follow certain levels of Japanese courtesy. The most well-known and common symbol of Japanese courtesy is the bow, commonly called the rei.

Judoka use the bow throughout the practice of judo to symbolize respect and to focus themselves for safe and serious practice. Reishiki begins when the judoka enters the dojo and bows to the dojo itself. Some schools have a picture of Jigoro Kano or the particular head of the school or association in the kamiza, upper seat, where the instructors sit, to which students bow before bowing to the mat and stepping onto the training surface.

Anytime a person sees a black belt or the instructor of the school, he or she should bow to that person as a matter of courtesy. The black belts will bow back to their students to show reciprocal respect.

A judo class bows to the instructor.

At the beginning of class, the students line up across from the instructor and all bow together to start the class. In the line, senior students are on the right with the ranks in descending order. If a large number of students are present, they form more than one line, with senior ranks in the front. When two students begin to work together, they usually bow to each other in respect and in preparation for earnest training.

Because judo training is based on combat techniques, carelessness in training can cause injury. It is important that students be resolute about their practice. Therefore, when getting ready to practice any of their skills, the judoka bow to each other as a sign of their serious intent to work together safely on the skills.

When practicing randori and when engaged in shiai, the two contestants bow to each other to show mutual respect, commitment to fair play, and serious intent to do their best to win. Although randori should not be about winning and losing, at least according to the teaching of Jigoro Kano, doing one's best is always expected of judoka.

Even shiai is supposed to have personal development as the first goal, ahead of the goal of winning. The idea of personal development means that a person learns to reach deep inside to find his or her best and express it in the contest.

When the bout, be it randori or shiai, is over, the two judoka again bow to each other to show respect and admiration, regardless of who won or lost. Respect is essential in the martial arts—without it, they are nothing more than violent activities or brutal sports.

When a judoka is having problems with a technique, he or she should ask questions. Some judo instructors believe that students need only to work through difficulties, whereas other instructors enjoy answering questions and helping students solve the riddle of technical proficiency. Students should ask questions and let the instructor address them as he or she wishes, whether through an answer or an admonition to practice more.

When students ask a question of a senior, they should begin with a bow and thank the instructor for helping, bowing again when the instruction is given.

Courtesy also extends to the way students treat each other. Judoka offer respect to both their seniors, those who outrank them, known in Japanese as *sempai,* and to their juniors, those of

The contestants bow to each other.

lesser rank, known in Japanese as *kohai*. Reishiki dictates that a person listens to and treats with respect those of higher ranks for having achieved what he or she aspires toward. A sempai is someone who has experience and knowledge from which others can learn and improve.

Judoka also owe a debt of gratitude to kohai, those in lower ranks. A sempai, someone with experience and knowledge, must share what he or she has learned with those coming up. Through the reishiki, cooperative courtesy between sempai and kohai, the art is preserved and progresses from one generation to the next.

Now that you have a working knowledge of a judo class, along with an understanding of basic terminology and courtesy, you can focus on the techniques required to perform the practice of judo. They can be found in chapters 4 through 9.

CHAPTER

4

FALLS AND ROLLS

kemi, or breakfalls, are essential to judo training. A student cannot practice judo safely until he or she learns to fall properly.

Ukemi skills are also necessary in competition. The judoka who is afraid to take a fall will be hesitant and tentative in the execution of throwing attacks during competition. As the old saying goes, "Those who hesitate are lost." Someone hesitant in competition cannot possibly be successful. Fear can often cause a person to be incapable of action. A judoka who does not have first-rate ukemi skills cannot possibly be bold in contest judo. The judoka must have immaculate martial-arts skills as well as absolute ability to receive falls. If a judoka is always worried about being thrown, the anxiety will create openings for a throw to occur. The person will hesitate in the execution of his or her technique, permitting the opponent to gain the upper hand.

Two main methods, slaps and rolls, are used in ukemi. When thrown, a judoka will make use of the slap in most techniques. The purpose of slapping the mat with the hand is to absorb most of the force by spreading the impact over a larger surface. When people without training fall, they generally stick out their arms to catch themselves. When they do so, all of their body weight focuses on the arm, producing a lot of stress along it. The stress causes damage, often in the form of a break. The correct technique will make the fall safer and less painful.

Another important part of falling correctly is tucking the head. Most serious injuries that occur in falls are caused by trauma to the head. In boxing the most severe injuries happen not when the boxer takes a blow to the head but when the boxer's head hits the

A judoka slaps the mat.

canvas after he has been knocked down. In judo, as well as in everyday life, the most important objective in a fall is to protect the head. One can best accomplish this by developing the habit of looking at the knot of the belt during ukemi training. When the judoka tucks the head in this manner, he or she can take all back and side falls safely. This position is also the proper one to use for rolls.

All judo instructors can tell stories from their own experience or from the experience of their students about how ukemi prevented serious injury after an accidental fall in everyday life. Slaps and rolls can protect a person from injury on the street. Although abrasions and bruises will result from a fall on concrete, people can avoid serious injury through proper ukemi.

PRACTICING FALLS

The safest way to practice ukemi skills is to begin with lying slaps. The judoka should lie on his or her back, with the knees up, and then slap the mat with the whole of the arms, making sure that the arms strike the mat from shoulder to fingertip, at a 45-degree angle to the torso. In all slaps the 45-degree angle is essential for maximum dissipation of force. The judoka should then lie on the right side, with the left knee up and the right leg slightly out. The judoka slaps the mat with just the right arm in the right-lying slap. He or she does the same on the left side, with the left leg slightly out and the right knee up, hitting the mat with just the left arm.

Another slap done from the lying position is the front slap. The judoka practices by lying on the abdomen, with the arms at a 45-degree angle. The person holds the head up, rather than tucked, so that it will not strike the mat when the person falls forward.

In the lying position the abdomen is on the mat, and the judoka focuses on hitting the mat solidly with both arms, with the palms facing the mat. In other forms of the front slap, the judoka bridges the body from knees to forearms or toes to forearms. Although rarely used in judo, the front slap has many practical applications in everyday life.

Once a student is proficient in lying slaps, he or she can progress to sitting slaps. Sitting on the floor, the student can practice slapping in two ways. First, he or she rolls back until the shoulder blades touch the mat. The student then slaps the surface and rolls back into the sitting position. The student performs the roll straight back, to the right, and to the left.

Second, the judoka rolls back until the shoulder blades touch the mat and then falls with the whole body, slapping with the feet and arms in the back slap and with the appropriate foot, leg, and arm in the right and left slaps.

Next, the judoka uses squatting slaps. In this position, the person falls backward, rolling back and hitting the mat with both arms. Then, to do the right slap, the judoka sticks out the right leg diagonally, causing a fall to the right and allowing performance of a right slap. The person performs the left slap by sticking out the left leg diagonally, so that the fall goes to the left and allows performance of a left slap.

The judoka can do a front slap from the squatting position by dropping to the knees, falling forward, holding the head up, bridging the body up between the knees, and striking the mat with the arms from elbows to fingertips, at a 45-degree angle relative to the head.

Next the judoka should practice these slaps from a standing position. To do a back slap, the judoka squats and rolls backward into the back slap and then rolls back up to a standing position. On each side, the judoka throws out the appropriate leg and falls to the side into a proper slap. A front slap can be done by falling forward and performing the proper slap. The student should not attempt the standing forward slap without achieving proficiency in the lying and squatting slaps.

ROLLS

After mastering the slaps, the judoka must learn how to perform rolls. The student can begin by rolling from a seated position, both forward and backward. The head must be tucked when performing all rolls. The judoka should practice rolling over both the left and right shoulders.

Although rolls are not often used in competition, the confidence they inspire in body manipulation adds much to the judoka's capability. Rolls occur often in self-defense situations. When pushed off balance, a person may use a roll to get away from an

TECHNIQUE TIPS FOR FALLS AND ROLLS

1. Begin practicing the most basic falls and rolls (closest to the mat) before progressing to the more difficult ones (standing) and always practice on a soft surface (mat, carpet, grass).
2. Relax your body throughout the fall or roll and remember to breathe out during impact.
3. Keep your chin tucked on all rolls and falls (except front fall).
4. Never extend a limb to break your fall, but instead allow your entire body to cushion the impact of the fall.
5. Remember to slap the mat with your whole arm and with the palm facing the mat as your back or side makes contact with the mat.

attacker and come immediately to his or her feet. Rolls can prevent injuries in everyday life. For example, if a person twists an ankle because of a hole or an uneven surface, he or she can use a roll to keep from putting weight on the ankle and breaking it.

After learning to perform the rolls from a sitting position, the judoka can practice the same rolls from a kneeling position and then from a squatting position. From there, the student learns to perform the rolls standing. Before progressing to the standing position, the student must be able to roll safely when sitting, kneeling, and squatting. Safety is paramount.

Standing rolls are generally practiced with the idea of the judoka rolling from the beginning standing position to another standing position. In this way the judoka learns to regain footing quickly.

ROLLING SLAPS

After learning how to roll and how to slap, the judoka can practice rolling slaps. The student starts into a roll but instead of rolling to the feet, he or she ends in a back or side slap. This skill is useful in the development of safe ukemi.

When a judoka can perform a rolling slap, he or she has come close to the experience of being thrown. Thus the judoka can work on safe falling skills even when a partner is not available. Rolling slaps help the judoka become accustomed to the sensation of going head over heels, an action that occurs in most throws. The practitioner can thus maintain mental equilibrium even while being thrown. If the opponent's throw does not score, the judoka still has a chance to win by being prepared for ground work once on the mat.

Once the judoka has mastered the basic breakfalls and rolls, the next step is for the instructor to throw the student in some gentle throws until the student is proficient in landing safely. The student can then take some throws at regular speed and strength.

This training sequence should give the judoka the confidence to perform in a competitive situation. The judoka must practice ukemi regularly to maintain skill and confidence.

LYING SLAP

Start by lying on your back with your knees bent and arms bent and crossed in front of you. To practice this basic ukemi, slap the mat (palm hitting mat) with your whole arm at a 45-degree angle relative to the torso and tuck your chin to your chest. Remember to exhale as you slap.

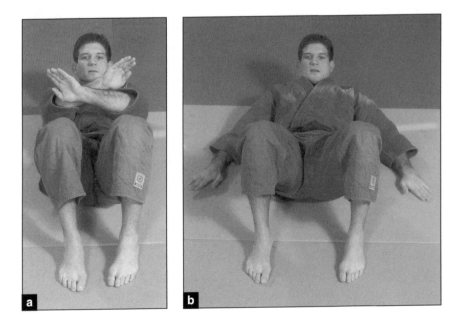

LYING SIDE SLAP

Start by lying on your right side with your right leg straight, your left knee up, and your right hand on your left hip. To execute the slap, bring your right hand off your hip and slap the mat with the palm of your hand and your arm at a 45-degree angle and make sure to raise your head off the mat. Exhale as you slap.

SITTING REAR SLAP

Start by sitting on the mat with your legs straight and your arms bent and crossed in front of you. Begin by rolling onto your back, allowing your legs to naturally rise to a 45-degree angle, and slap with both arms the moment your shoulder blades touch the mat. Remember to keep your chin tucked to prevent you from banging your head and exhale as you slap.

RIGHT SQUATTING SLAP

From a squatting position, straighten and then swing your right leg diagonally to your left and bring your right hand to the left side of your body. This will cause you to begin to fall to the right. As your body hits the mat, slap firmly with your right arm at a 45-degree angle and keep your legs from crossing. Remember to keep your chin tucked and exhale as you slap.

STANDING REAR SLAP

This technique is similar to the sitting rear slap. It is done by starting from a standing position to increase the momentum of the fall and increase your proficiency in the technique. Start standing and begin to squat down by bending your knees (similar to sitting in an imaginary chair). As you do this cross your arms in front of you. Continue sitting until your buttocks touch the mat and then roll onto your back allowing your legs to rise naturally into the air and keeping your chin tucked. Slap with the palms of both of your hands as your shoulder blades make contact with the mat and exhale as you slap. You must first perfect the sitting rear slap technique before advancing to the standing rear slap.

STANDING FRONT SLAP

Although this technique is rarely used in judo practice or competition, it is excellent to know for injury prevention in real-life situations. To practice the fall, start standing then begin to fall forward (toward your abdomen), bending your knees as you fall. Kick your legs back and bring your arms in front of you at a 45-degree angle to catch you as you fall. When you make contact with the mat, slap with your forearms and palms of your hands and hold your head up and to the side, rather than tucked, to prevent it from hitting the ground. In the finish position, only your arms and feet should be in contact with the mat.

FRONT ROLLING SLAP

From a standing position, take one step forward with your right foot. Place your left hand with palm down onto the mat for balance (fingertips facing away from you), then curl your right arm in toward your body and swing it through your legs (fingertips facing you). Tuck your head and roll forward over your right shoulder and swing your left leg into the air. As you come out of the roll, you should end up on your left side and slap the mat with your left palm. Exhale as you slap the mat to break your fall. The correct finishing position will have you lying on your left side, left palm striking the mat, feet apart, and head off the mat.

The front rolling breakfall is similar to a gymnastics forward somersault, but it is done diagonally across the back rather than head-on.

Remember to practice this ukemi on both sides as you never know to which side you will be thrown.

a

You must practice proper ukemi every day, devoting some time in each training session to proper falling techniques. Once you master these skills, you are ready to work on subsequent judo skills with self-assurance and confidence.

CHAPTER

5

STANCES AND GRIPS

t is impossible to do good judo without using stances and grips correctly. All throws begin with a good stance and a proper grip, and all chokes, joint locks, and holds depend on solid grips. Students should study these important fundamentals of judo thoroughly.

STANCES

Judo stresses complete naturalness in stance and movement. The first posture a judo student learns is *shizentai,* sometimes also known as *shizen hontai.* Both terms mean "natural body." In shizentai the feet are shoulder-width apart, and the weight is evenly distributed over the feet. If the judoka steps forward with the left foot, the stance is called *hidari shizentai.* If the right foot is forward, the stance is known as *migi shizentai,* which is the most fundamental posture in judo. Everything else revolves around shizentai.

TECHNIQUE TIPS FOR STANCES

1. Shizentai, or natural posture, is an upright stance with the feet about shoulder-width apart. Whether attacking or defending, try to maintain this stance.

2. When fighting, avoid the natural tendency to crouch and bend. Doing so will only reduce your mobility and make you more vulnerable to being thrown.

3. Keep your back straight, hold your head up, and move around with your feet always about shoulder-width apart.

4. Never cross your feet or bring them too close together because doing so will lead to a loss of stability.

5. When moving around, maintain a relaxed manner, keeping your feet close to the ground.

The second stance is *jigotai,* also known as *jigo hontai,* which literally means "self-defense body." In this situation, the feet are about twice shoulder-width apart, and the weight is evenly distributed over the feet. As in the first posture, if the left foot is forward the stance becomes *hidari jigotai,* and if the right foot is forward the stance is *migi jigotai.*

These six stances form the fighting foundation of judo. All movements from shizentai moving left and right and from jigotai moving left and right are transitory. Kano taught that a person assumed jigotai only to block an attack or add impetus to a throw. A good judoka never simply assumes jigotai because it is not a primary stance. The practitioner flows in and out of jigotai without hesitation.

Three other positions that should be noted are anza, seiza, and kyoshi no kamae. *Anza* is relaxed sitting, which means sitting on the floor with the legs crossed. This is the common way of sitting in the dojo.

Seiza, which literally means "right sitting," is the formal Japanese sitting position. One sits with the hips upon one's heels. Judoka use this position most of the time and perform the formal sitting bow, *zarei,* in this position. Seiza is used when kneeling and should be well developed, but when sitting becomes uncomfortable it is permissible to switch to the anza position.

Finally, the *kyoshi no kamae* is the kneeling position in which one knee is on the ground, the body is raised, and the other foot is flat on the ground. Kyoshi no kamae is used in some kata as a method of posture from which certain moves are practiced. Judoka also use kyoshi no kamae in the practice of many rear chokes.

When standing up from seiza, the idea is to move from the sitting position to the raised posture of kyoshi no kamae and then to a standing posture, usually shizentai. Although these three positions are not actually stances, the serious judoka should master them.

NATURAL POSTURE

For *shizen hontai,* stand normally with your back straight and knees slightly bent. Place your feet shoulder-width apart and keep your weight evenly distributed over your feet. This is also known as shizentai.

SELF-DEFENSE POSTURE

For *jigotai* start standing normally. Spread your feet to double shoulder-width apart, bending your knees while keeping your back straight. Let your arms hang with fisted hands near your inner thigh regions.

RELAXED SITTING POSTURE

Anza is relaxed sitting, which means sitting on the floor with the legs crossed. This is the common way of sitting in the dojo, especially for long periods of time.

RIGHT SITTING POSTURE

Seiza is the formal Japanes sitting position. From shizentai, kneel down onto your left knee first then your right, keeping your back straight throughout. Sit back onto your heels (hips touching heels) and place your hands on your lap with fingertips facing slightly inward.

KNEELING POSTURE

Kyoshi no kamae is the kneeling position where one knee is on the ground while the body is raised and the other foot is flat on the ground. This is a common position for practice of shime waza, and it is also employed during kata.

GRIPS

A judoka must know how to grip an opponent properly. In judo, primarily a grappling art, the ability to connect with and control an opponent begins with a proper grip. Without a proper, solid grip, one will lose the hold and be unable to break an opponent's balance, perform skillful chokes, or maintain a hold or joint lock for the required time. Without a good grip, judo does not work. The *kumi kata* is the basic grip used for practicing throwing skills.

The kumi kata has the right hand gripping the left lapel of the opponent and the left hand gripping the right sleeve above the elbow. In the old days of the Kodokan, it was common for two judoka to come to grips in this fashion at the beginning of randori and shiai. Some judo organizations not connected to the Olympic judo forum still require this beginning. In modern sport judo, however, competitors have a tendency to "fight" for a favorable handhold. Thus a judoka should master all the handholds that can be beneficial in contest judo.

Those interested in self-defense should note that these kumi kata, forms of gripping, are important to actual combat. In the use of judo techniques as self-defense, the judoka must be able to establish a grip that will create an advantage and allow the execution of a successful counterattack.

In the realm of competition, a good grip allows the judoka to move directly into a throw, choke, or joint lock. Several kumi kata are taught in basic judo.

The basic grip is useful for both competition and self-defense. For the reverse grip, the left hand grips the right lapel while the right hand grips the left sleeve. This grip is especially useful for left-handed people.

An unusual grip used by some judoka is to grab the opponent by the seam area where the sleeves go into the rest of the jacket area on the uwagi. This can be a strong grip, but one must exercise it carefully to gain the initiative and execute a throw.

In the explanation of the following grips, one should keep in mind that the great master Kazuzo Kudo, a personal student of Jigoro Kano, says that the judoka should always seek to grip the arm on the side of the direction of the throw. This position gives better leverage and control of the opponent, while keeping the gripping arm of the judoka safe. When the arm is anywhere else in the execution of a technique, there is a great danger of that arm being damaged in the fall.

As the following grips are being explained, keep in mind that as one arm takes the location being described, the other hand grabs the opposing arm, usually above the elbow.

Many judoka, especially those engaged in a match with a shorter opponent, find that gripping the collar behind the neck is an excellent strategy. This grip greatly improves the leverage that the judoka can direct against a challenger.

Some judoka grip the lapel up close to the neck where they can direct the pressure of the grip against the neck itself. Some instructors teach that when gripping an opponent the hands should never be placed higher on the competitor's body than one's own shoulders. Although this is true for throws that use *tsurikomi,* or a lift pull, it is not necessarily true for all throws. Therefore this is a sound rule if a judoka is applying a throw using tsurikomi, but it is not a general principle for all throws.

Some judoka, depending on whether they are taller or shorter than the opponent, like to reach over the shoulder of the opponent or under the armpit to grasp the back of the jacket. But if the competitor has mastered the *makikomi,* or wraparound throws, this can be a risky strategy.

Some judoka like to assume jigotai, the self-defense posture, in which the feet are about twice shoulder-width apart. Then, in the standard grip, they put the right arm into the opponent's left armpit while using the left hand to grab the right arm above the elbow. This form of gripping dates back to old jujutsu schools and was used against an opponent wielding a short sword or knife. When mastered, this grip can be extremely effective in competition and even in self-defense.

In general, different grips on sleeves, lapels, and other places on the uwagi, or jacket, are essential to good throwing skills. One other method of kumi kata involves gripping the obi, or belt. This is often referred to as *obi tori,* belt taking.

The great Japanese judo champion Katsuhiko Kashiwazaki developed a variety of ways of gripping the belt. He modified many of his throws to accommodate his special obi tori methods, which turned into a winning strategy that helped him be a great champion.

The manner of gripping with the hand in these kumi kata is important. The most common mistake that beginning judoka make is gripping too tightly with the whole hand. This immobilizes the hand, making it less capable of performing the subtle moves necessary to execute good judo techniques. When the hand is held tightly all the time, the hand and arm may become fatigued, leading to failure of the limb during competition.

The grip used in judo is the same as that used for holding a *katana*, the samurai sword. The little finger, ring finger, and, according to some, the middle finger grip firmly. The index finger and thumb hold lightly. At the point of execution, the whole hand grips strongly. Before that instant, however, a hand gripped too tightly will be a hindrance to the judoka.

The light hand allows for sensitivity to the movements of the opponent. This is literally an expression of the principle of ju. The soft hand allows an experienced judoka to sense the movements of an opponent—to perceive what is coming and counter it, or to feel a moment of weakness or hesitation and then execute a technique.

BASIC GRIP

Grab opponent's left lapel (at chest level) with your right hand and grip his or her right sleeve above the elbow with your left hand.

In the old Kodokan days, this basic grip was the starting point for judoka during both randori and shiai; however, it is very rare to see this grip used in competition today because competitors have a tendency to "fight" for a favorable handhold.

BASIC LEFT-HANDED GRIP

Grab opponent's right lapel (at chest level) with your left hand and take hold of his or her left sleeve (near his wrist) with your right hand. For right-handed judoka, everything is the exact opposite as described above.

This is one of the most common grips used in competition today. The ideal situation is for you to have both of your hands on your opponent as described above while he or she only has one hand on your judo gi.

ARMPIT GRIP

With your right hand grab the left side of opponent's jacket where the sleeve meets the rest of the jacket (armpit area) and take hold of opponent's right sleeve (near the wrist) with your left hand.

This grip gives you excellent control of your opponent's upper body; however, it is rarely seen in high-caliber judo competitions due to the tightness of the uniforms used in competition today.

HIGH RIGHT COLLAR GRIP

Take hold of opponent's right sleeve with your left hand (near the wrist) and grab the collar area behind the neck of your opponent with your right hand.

This grip is typically used by judoka who are taller than their opponents because it is a more comfortable grip and it improves one's leverage.

BELT GRIP

Once you have your opponent's right sleeve with your left hand, reach under his or her left arm and around the back with your right hand and grab the belt (near the middle).

The belt grip is perhaps the strongest grip in judo as it provides maximum control of your opponent's upper body. Against an experienced judoka this grip will be hard to attain, and always keep in mind that once you have grabbed your opponent's belt you must attack in 3 to 5 seconds. Failure to do so will result in a penalty of *shido*.

LIGHT HAND GRIP

This figure demonstrates the proper way the hand is supposed to hold the sleeve of your opponent's judo gi. Rather than making a tight fist around the gi, the gi is held firmly between the thumb and first two fingers. This is sometimes referred to as the "light hand grip." Employing this method will delay the fatigue felt by your forearms while holding the gi.

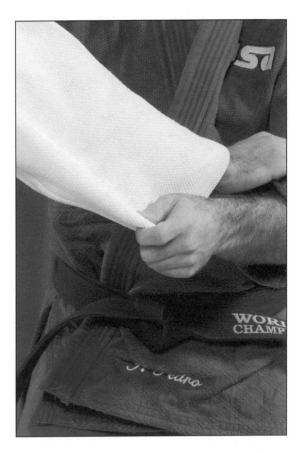

Stances and grips are extremely important aspects of judo. The judoka should study them thoroughly as an entry into all judo skills.

CHAPTER
6

THROWS

*N*age *waza*, throwing techniques, are the primary techniques of Kodokan judo. This aspect of judo makes up the primary skills that are practiced in randori (sparring) and then applied in shiai (competition). When Jigoro Kano began his training in jujutsu many years ago, his first love was throwing. Samurai who fought in armor developed throwing as the primary skills of jujutsu because punches and kicks would not work well against people whose vital points were covered. But even warriors wearing armor could be thrown with proper skill. Foot soldiers wore a light set of armor, making it possible to use all the throws common to jujutsu against them.

Under his Kito Ryu instructor, Kano discovered the key to throwing, the use of *kuzushi,* the balance-breaking principle. With an understanding of this principle, Kano became almost unthrowable. Kano developed the idea of breaking a person's balance and then, with proper timing, moving into a throw so that the person was helpless to resist it. Kano thus developed the three essential aspects of the throw—kuzushi, *tsukuri* (positioning), and *kake* (the throw itself).

Kano prized throwing more than he did any other skill of judo. He found in throwing a challenge and an aesthetic quality not

TECHNIQUE TIPS FOR THROWS

1. The three basic elements to any judo throw are kuzushi, tsukuri, and kake.

2. Each judo throw has a unique grip or hand placement. Before you begin to learn a throw, make sure that your hands are in the right place.

3. Kuzushi, or off balancing your opponent, is the most important element to a successful throw. Make sure to use the proper kuzushi for each throwing technique.

4. Tsukuri, or timing, is the next important element of a successful throw. Pay close attention to the proper foot, hip, or leg placement for each throw.

5. Repetition is the key to perfecting any judo technique. Performing many uchikomi, or fit-ins, will ensure mastery of both kuzushi and tsukuri.

6. The final element of any throw is kake, or finish of the technique. Doing nagekomi, throwing without resistance, is an excellent way to perfect kake.

7. Always maintain good posture when executing a throw.

8. Try to perfect a few techniques with which you can throw any opponent rather than learning to perform many techniques only adequately.

9. When a particular technique is ineffective, go back to the basics to determine what you are doing wrong.

found in other forms of training. In addition, Kano wanted a method of safe practice that would allow spontaneity yet guard against injury. As he developed his form of randori, he emphasized the techniques of throwing, excluding skills he thought might cause injury to his students. From 1882 until 1900, judo contests were primarily throwing contests, a skill at which the judoka trained by Kano excelled.

Kano originally intended judo to be a standing martial art, an art that emphasized throwing skills and included no mat work. The great master and founder of Kodokan judo was so accomplished at throwing that people said battling him was like fighting an empty jacket. Kano had such great skill in yielding that it felt as if he were not there, as if he offered no resistance to push or pull against. This was a great compliment, indicating how completely Kano had mastered the principle of ju.

THREE PHASES OF THROWING

While learning *nage waza,* throwing techniques, the beginning judoka is taught that each throw consists of three parts—kuzushi, tsukuri, and kake. Kuzushi refers to balance breaking, the first and most essential part of a throw. Developing this skill marked Kano's entry into mastery of judo.

Two sets of kuzushi are commonly taught in judo. The first is called *roppo no kuzushi,* the six directions of breaking, which refers to left, right, forward left, forward right, back left, and back right. The second set is *happo no kuzushi,* the eight directions of breaking, which adds movements directly forward and backward to the other six.

One can practice alone moving in these directions, using the *tsugi ashi* footwork. But it is essential to practice the concept of kuzushi with a partner. When performing the kuzushi, the student

The first stage of throwing, kuzushi.

uses subtle pressure to lead and guide the partner in the various directions. To become skilled at throwing, the judoka must learn how to break a person's balance to set up the person for the throw. When the student develops proper kuzushi, little effort is required to execute a throw. This ability is the essence of judo, according to Jigoro Kano.

Kuzushi is important not only in sport but also in self-defense. In sport one expects to compete against a person of similar size, but in self-defense a person generally faces an attack by a larger or stronger opponent. To offset this disadvantage, the expert in judo uses kuzushi, a manifestation of the principle of ju, to lead the attacker into a weakened position. At that juncture the judoka can more easily overcome the assailant.

Once kuzushi is accomplished, the next stage in throwing is tsukuri. In some ways, and particularly in some throws, tsukuri is possibly the most important aspect. The body of the thrower

The second stage of throwing, tsukuri.

$\int$ELF-DEFENSE TIPS

In self-defense situations, a judo throw can be a devastating way to deal with an assailant. A throw can cause serious injury to someone who does not know how to fall properly or to someone who is thrown onto the street. The key to executing a judo throw in this situation is to close the gap between you and your assailant. The skilled judoka who accomplishes this will always have the upper hand.

1. Do not hesitate. Grab the assailant, react quickly, and attack (enter into a throw) fast and hard.

2. Avoid using throws that roll the opponent to the ground and beware of using sacrifice throws because in self-defense situations you should stay on your feet.

3. Intensify your technique by not holding on to the assailant as he falls. The assailant will hit the ground harder and in a more uncontrolled manner.

4. Look to follow through with submission techniques, such as armlocks and chokes. Armlocks need to be secured if they are to be effective. If you do not put the arm out of action, the attacker can continue the attack.

5. If multiple attackers are present, finish with striking, so that you stay on your feet.

6. Practice judo occasionally with someone who is not wearing a judo gi to prepare yourself for the real-world situation in which your attacker is not wearing a jacket.

must move into a position that permits the leverage of the particular technique to be effective.

The three main methods of throwing are known in judo as *koshi waza*, *ashi waza*, and *te waza*, which mean, respectively, hip techniques, foot or leg techniques, and hand techniques. To produce an effective throw, the thrower uses the hip, the foot or the leg, or the hand to block or obstruct some part of the body of the receiver.

At this point the throw comes to fruition in the kake. Although kake literally means "attack," it refers to the actual completion of the throw, when the receiver is hurled to the ground. In competitive judo, the thrower either holds on to the opponent's sleeve as the receiver hits the ground or goes to the ground with the receiver to work a *ne waza,* lying technique. In self-defense, circumstances vary, but it is possible to do the throw without holding on so that the assailant hits the ground harder. In situations where the judoka feels more in control, he or she can hold on to the attacker to keep the attacker from hitting the ground too hard.

In some throws the three stages happen in order, one following the other—kuzushi, breaking the balance; tsukuri, positioning for the throw; and kake, the throw. On other occasions the kuzushi and tsukuri occur simultaneously, with the kake following. In some throws the three phases happen simultaneously. Finally, in a few throws the tsukuri happens first, the kuzushi occurs next, and the kake ends the technique.

The key to great judo is learning how to apply these three phases of throwing. Successful throwing is the greatest of all concepts of judo and is essentially the physical application of ju.

The third stage of throwing, kake.

Gaining kuzushi can be passive, as when the opponent attacks with a push or pull or even a strike. In this situation, the judoka blends with the movement, using the momentum of the assault to lead the opponent into a throw.

When the opponent does not attack, as in the sport aspect of judo, the competitor uses a slight push or pull—that is, some form of an attack—to elicit a reaction from the opponent. As the opponent responds with either a push or a pull, the process becomes one of blending with the force of the reaction, again leading into kuzushi and a technique. This action is known as *hando no kuzushi,* pressure movement.

The student practices each throw standing still, with an emphasis on mastering the three fundamental aspects of nage waza—kuzushi, tsukuri, and kake.

As a precursor to randori, the judoka practices moving with a partner, taking two or three steps in the appropriate direction for the application of the particular throw he or she wants to perform. The judoka works on kuzushi especially but strives for mastery of all aspects of the throw.

It is essential that a judoka master the concepts of *taisabaki* (body movement) and kuzushi, along with their related principles. If the student does not master these concepts, he or she will never become truly effective in throwing.

With mastery of these principles, however, a person can develop superior skill and capability. A champion of judo has practiced these skills so thoroughly that they are second nature. The master judoka applies these concepts intuitively, leading to successful performance in competition or self-defense.

METHODS OF PRACTICING THROWS

Throws can be practiced in two ways. In complete form, the judoka throws the partner to the ground. Practiced in form only, commonly known as *uchikomi,* the emphasis is on developing the skills of kuzushi (balance breaking) and tsukuri (body positioning). In uchikomi the judoka practices the throw only up to the point of the actual throw. In this way the student can perfect kuzushi and tsukuri without wearing out the training partner. The judoka may set up a throw 10 times and then throw once. Generally, if the uchikomi is perfect, the throw will be perfect. In many judo schools more time is spent on uchikomi than on actual throwing. When practiced with a partner, uchikomi is called *sotai renshu.*

Uchikomi can also be practiced without a partner, a method known as *tandoku renshu uchikomi.* Here the judoka stands in the position of practicing the throws and goes through the movements of performing the technique. For example, if the judoka is practicing ogoshi, the major hip throw, he or she will step with the right foot into the position of the throw and then turn so that the left foot moves into parallel position. Finally, the practitioner moves the arms through the movements of throwing the imaginary opponent over the hips.

The student should practice these repetitions often. It is always best to work with a partner, but individual practice is important and, unfortunately, often neglected by many modern judoka.

After students have spent considerable time mastering the basic throws, they can then be worked in kata. In judo, kata is a prearranged set of movements performed by a pair of judoka. One is the *tori,* the person doing the skills, the other is the *uke,* the person receiving the techniques. The primary kata for mastering throws, especially for use in randori and shiai, is nage no kata, the first half of the forms known collectively as *randori no kata.*

Finally, to master throws for competition, the judoka must spend time in randori. Some randori can be engaged in just as throwing exercises, which is a good way to master throws. Whereas kata teaches the form of the throws and helps a person master the principles involved, randori, because it is a freestyle movement, allows the judoka to develop the spontaneity needed to use the throws in competition or self-defense. The martial artist needs some method of extemporaneous practice to be able to use skills spontaneously. This is the rationale for randori.

Randori can be practiced in several ways. First, the players can take turns throwing with little resistance. Next, the two judoka can practice only certain throws or one of them can call out the name of the throw he or she is going to attempt. Third, judoka can practice randori as a method of working on counters. One partner starts a throw, and the other works on countering or blocking the throw. Fourth, the players can offer a little more resistance but still keep randori more an exercise than a competition. Finally, there is a competitive form of randori, which resembles a shiai, a contest, though with less intensity.

Except in shiai, the judoka should not use full effort, especially in randori practice. Kano always taught that winning should not be the most important goal of randori, or even shiai. The main goal is learning. Sometimes it is impossible to learn when one is consumed with competition.

Randori should be a time when a person learns the intricacies of throwing, especially the triune principles of kuzushi, tsukuri, and kake. Randori is a practice method, not a competition. Although one should never throw a match or do less than his or her best, a judoka should not become obsessed with winning to the point of forgetting the reason for randori, learning.

For each of the three basic types of throws—forward, backward, and sideways—there are many variations one can use to throw an opponent. One throw may look like another at first, but different handholds (grips) or foot positions distinguish them. In addition, all the techniques of judo can be done on both the left and right sides.

Although all of the following techniques are broken down into stages, a throw takes only a second or two to accomplish. Most successful throws are but a brief explosion in which the judoka performs all the stages simultaneously. To learn the techniques, the student starts by standing still and then walks through each stage in slow motion, focusing on the mechanics of the throw. The instructor should make sure that the student is doing the technique properly. The student then repeats the throw many times until he or she can do all three stages in one easy motion. Next, the student attempts the throw while moving in the direction of the intended throw. The student should find it easier to throw while moving. In class, students will take turns being tori and uke so that they learn both how to throw the opponent and how to defend against a throw.

FORWARD THROWS

A number of different forward throws are used in judo. The judoka typically uses forward throws when the opponent is pushing on the judoka or walking forward. With proper timing, tori can use uke's weight or forward momentum to his or her advantage, give way, and then throw uke. The following five forward techniques are the most popular ones used in judo today. Although all the techniques demonstrated in this book are done on the left side, the throws may also be done on the right.

MAJOR HIP THROW

Ogoshi, major hip throw, is usually the first throw taught to beginners because it is the easiest throw to perform against someone who is not resisting. Ogoshi also teaches the novice judoka all the concepts of executing a judo throw, including kuzushi, tsukuri, and kake.

Tori first grabs uke's left sleeve with the right hand and reaches around uke's waist to grab the belt or back with the left hand. Tori then pulls with the right hand and steps in front of uke's left foot

with the left foot. Tori pivots on the left foot and swings the right foot around so that the feet are shoulder-width apart and facing in the same direction as uke's feet. The knees should be slightly bent. To finish, tori straightens the legs, twists to the right, and swings uke over the hips and down to the mat.

SWEEPING HIP THROW

Haraigoshi, sweeping hip throw, is typically a throw that a bigger, heavier person uses against a smaller opponent. In attempting haraigoshi, the thrower will often feel the opponent begin to fall and throw his or her own weight down to the mat to complete the throw. Extra weight is an advantage to the thrower in this variation, called *harai-makikomi*.

Tori first grabs uke's collar with the left hand and uke's sleeve with the right hand. Tori then pulls with both hands, pulling uke's sleeve high toward the chest and placing the left foot in front of uke's left foot. Tori pivots on the left foot and places the right foot (with leg bent slightly) between uke's feet. The left leg sweeps uke's leg so that uke begins to fall. To finish, tori straightens the right leg and pulls hard on uke's sleeve hand while the left leg throws uke to the mat.

a

INNER LEG REAP

Uchimata, inner leg reap, is a spectacular and dynamic technique. It requires an incredible amount of skill and talent to perfect. Uchimata is most often done against an opponent who is bent over or whose legs are spread wide apart.

First, tori grabs uke's collar with the left hand and grabs uke's left sleeve with the right. Tori then pulls uke's sleeve hand up toward the chest and steps in front of uke's left foot with the left foot. Next, tori pivots off the left foot and back steps deeply with the right foot, placing it between uke's legs and keeping it slightly bent. Tori transfers weight onto the right foot, continues to pull with the hands, and lifts uke with the hips. To finish, tori straightens the right leg and swings the left leg up and between uke's legs while turning the head to the right. Tori then throws uke to the mat.

SHOULDER THROW

Seionage, shoulder throw, is a relatively easy throw to learn that is usually taught in the early stages of judo. This throw is usually done against a larger opponent. By dropping down on the knees (not illustrated), the judoka can perform the throw more easily because he or she does not have to pick up the opponent. Performing the throw standing up, however, will typically result in a much higher score.

Tori first grabs uke's right lapel with the left hand and grabs the left sleeve with the right hand. Tori pulls uke's sleeve hand toward himself or herself and steps with the left foot in front of uke's left foot, simultaneously bringing the left arm across uke's body and tucking it under uke's armpit. Tori turns the left hip into uke by pivoting on the left foot and swinging the right foot around so that the feet are shoulder-width apart and facing in the same direction as uke's feet. The legs should be slightly bent. To finish, tori straightens the legs to lift uke off his or her feet, pulls with the arms, rotates to the right, and throws uke to the mat.

BODY DROP

Taiotoshi, body drop, is a difficult throw to master, even for the advanced judoka. With this technique, timing and speed are crucial for success. It differs from ogoshi and seionage in that the judoka does not have to lift the opponent with the hips to throw. Instead, tori trips uke over the leg using uke's momentum.

Tori takes a sleeve grip with the right hand and a lapel grip with the left hand. To start the throw, tori pulls uke's sleeve away from uke's body. Tori steps diagonally with the left foot inside uke's right foot and has the weight on the ball of the foot. Tori pivots off the left foot and swings the right foot around, placing it outside uke's right foot. Tori places the left foot outside uke's left foot and transfers body weight onto the left foot. Both feet should be outside uke's legs. To finish, tori pulls on uke's sleeve, pushes with the lapel hand, and throws uke to the mat.

BACKWARD THROWS

Judo practitioners use a number of backward throws. A judoka typically uses backward throws when the opponent is pulling him or her or the opponent is bent over leaning to the rear. Two of the most common backward throws are *osotogari* and *ouchigari*.

MAJOR OUTER REAPING

For *osotogari,* major outer reaping, tori grabs uke's sleeve with the right hand and the lapel or neck with the left hand. Tori takes a step forward with the right foot (next to uke's left foot) and hooks the outside of uke's left leg with the left leg. While controlling uke with the hands and transferring most of uke's weight over the left leg, tori then sweeps the left leg back, taking uke's feet off the mat. Tori throws uke down to the mat by continuing to lift the left leg and bending the upper body toward the mat.

MAJOR INNER REAPING

Ouchigari, major inner reaping, is one of the most popular backward techniques. This throw complements seionage and taiotoshi well.

Tori holds uke's sleeve with the right hand and uke's lapel with the left hand. Tori starts to pull uke with the hands as if to make a forward throw. Tori then steps into uke with the right foot, turns the left hip towards uke, and hooks uke's right leg with the left leg. Tori sweeps uke's right leg away in a circular motion with the left leg and pushes into uke, throwing uke to the mat.

SACRIFICE THROWS

Sutemi waza, or self-sacrifice throws, involve dropping to the mat in order to throw. The effectiveness of these techniques results from the thrower suddenly dropping his or her weight to the mat, causing the opponent to become off balance.

CIRCLE THROW

Tomoenage, circle throw, is often seen on television and the movies and is perhaps the most recognizable judo technique. The judoka typically uses tomoenage against a stiff opponent who is bending forward and pushing away with rigid arms. Tomoenage can be used against a considerably larger or taller opponent.

Tori takes a traditional grip, holding uke's sleeve with the right hand and the lapel with the left hand. As tori pulls up with both hands, he or she takes a step forward with the left foot and drops under uke by squatting down and placing the right foot on uke's abdomen. Tori pulls down with the hands, lifts uke with the right leg, and throws uke onto the mat so that uke lands over tori's head (with the path describing a full circle).

SHOULDER WHEEL

Katagaruma, shoulder wheel, is a modified version of the firefighter's carry used in wrestling. In the nage no kata this technique is shown standing up with a traditional two-handed grip. Done this way, only extremely strong judoka can perform the technique because the thrower must lift the opponent completely off the mat. A more practical way to perform the technique is illustrated here. This version of katagaruma is widely used in international competition. In this case, the thrower drops to the knees and attacks when the opponent has only one hand on the gi.

As uke grabs tori's collar or lapel with the right hand, tori comes inside and over the top of uke's arm with the left hand and grabs uke's gi behind the triceps. Next, tori steps with the left leg extended outside uke's right leg and ducks the head under uke's

right arm. Tori pulls down with the left arm and brings the right arm through uke's legs. Finally, tori throws uke to the mat by falling to the left and continuing to pull down with the left hand while lifting through uke's legs with the right hand.

a

SIDE THROWS

In Japanese, *ashi waza* means "foot and ankle techniques." Ashi waza, or foot sweeps, are one of the easiest ways to throw an opponent of any size. The timing of the technique is the most important element of a successful foot sweep. Ashi waza is also a useful way to set up an opponent for a major throw.

ADVANCING FOOT SWEEP

De ashi harai, advancing foot sweep, is typically used when both judoka are moving sideways. Tori uses a standard grip with the left hand on the lapel and the right hand on uke's sleeve. To start, tori must be half a step behind uke. As uke moves to tori's right, tori takes a quick step to the right and with the left foot sweeps uke's right ankle, making sure to stand tall with the hips into the throw. As tori sweeps uke's foot, tori pulls down with the lapel hand and up with the sleeve hand (similar to how one steers a car). As uke's right foot leaves the mat, tori lets go of the sleeve hand and throws uke to the mat.

As you learn the curriculum of judo throws, you will probably develop an affinity for a certain movement. It is best to cultivate this affinity into a *tokui waza,* a "favorite technique." Most judoka have two or three tokui waza that they can use at any moment. The idea is to develop skill in these techniques to such a high level that an opponent cannot stop them.

Once you have mastered the idea of throwing, you will begin to do mat work, which will be covered in the next two chapters. But you must be sure that you have mastered all the basic principles of throwing. Without the ability to drop an opponent, your ground skills may avail you nothing. Even if you choose to be a ne waza specialist, you must first get your opponent to the ground and be in an advantageous position to apply your ground-fighting skills.

CHAPTER

7

HOLDS AND PINS

*T*he second division of randori techniques are the *ne waza,* lying techniques. This division is also known as *katame waza,* or holding techniques. The three branches of ne waza are *osaekomi waza, shime waza,* and *kansetsu waza.* This chapter deals with *osaekomi waza,* pinning techniques, and the following chapter will cover the other two.

The first branch of ne waza for use as randori skills are the pinning techniques, designed to take control of one arm and the torso. In these techniques the judoka holds an opponent by immobilizing at least one arm while pinning the opponent to the ground through "pressure into" (the literal translation of osaekomi) the upper body. The techniques are based on grappling skills that were designed to deal with an attacker armed with a sword. The judoka immobilized the primary sword arm and controlled the body so that the opponent could not mount an effective defense.

When the techniques are practiced today, the judoka can immobilize either arm, although some of the *koryu,* ancient

TECHNIQUE TIPS FOR HOLDS AND PINS

1. Think ahead and look for a pin during the transition from standing to ground fighting.

2. For all hold-downs make sure that your opponent is carrying the majority of your body weight.

3. Be sure to keep your legs a safe distance from your opponents' legs to avoid entanglement, which voids the pin.

4. Try to anticipate your opponent's next move so that you will be able to react when it occurs.

5. Change your pin only when it is necessary to do so (when your opponent is going to escape for sure).

6. Practice escaping from pins in case you ever find yourself in one. Doing this will also help you understand what your opponent might do when you are applying a pin.

systems, still preserve the traditional way of practicing by holding the sword arm under control. In judo competition what matters most is controlling the opponent.

Originally, the pins were designed to give the defender leverage to break the sword arm or choke the attacker into submission. When Kano modified the techniques so that his students could safely practice them in competition, he made them a matter of skill and control rather than a way to attack the arm or throat.

To score a point in competitive judo, a pin must be held for a full 25 seconds. Control of the arm and torso is essential to scoring in competition. If a competitor holds a pin for 20 seconds before the opponent breaks it, a half point is awarded.

A competitor scores points by holding the opponent on the opponent's back. The competitor must control the opponent's head and maintain chest-to-chest contact.

Osaekomi waza are among the most strenuous techniques in judo. It takes a great deal of strength, skill, and endurance to hold the pin for the full time.

Although a limited number of techniques are used as osaekomi waza, the potential variations are numerous. These techniques are good methods for entering into other techniques, such as chokes or joint locks.

Osaekomi waza techniques are valuable for the judoka because they can end a match. When the judoka masters ground-work skills, he or she can avoid trouble after being brought down to the mat by a bad throw or a movement from the opponent. The judoka skilled in osaekomi waza can easily regain the initiative.

Considerable time and effort are required to develop osaekomi waza. By starting on the ground, judoka can perform randori to work exclusively on these techniques. One method of ground randori begins with the judoka sitting back to back. At the command to begin, the players spin around and begin to work on their ground-fighting techniques.

While working osaekomi waza, judoka should master escapes and defenses against these techniques, known as *nogare kata* and *fusegi,* respectively. As a student learns each osaekomi, he or she should study the appropriate escape and defense.

UPPER FOUR-SIDE HOLD

Kamishihogatame is perhaps the strongest hold-down in judo because it is the most difficult hold from which to escape. Tori starts by lying on top of uke so that tori's head and chest are over uke's chest. Tori's abdomen and hips must be low and flat and the feet spread wide. Tori slides both arms along the mat, under uke's shoulders, and grasps uke's belt on both sides. Tori tightens the hold by squeezing the elbows together and pulling uke's belt toward himself or herself.

SIDE FOUR-SIDE HOLD

For *yokoshihogatame* tori starts by lying perpendicular to uke with his or her chest on uke's chest. Tori takes the right arm around and under uke's head and grabs the collar on the far side. Tori passes the left arm through uke's thighs and grasps uke's belt, or skirt of the gi on the other side. The hips must be low and the feet spread apart.

VERTICAL FOUR-SIDE HOLD

Tateshihogatame begins with uke lying on his or her back and tori lying on top of uke. Tori's head faces uke's head. Tori hooks his or her legs outside uke's legs and wraps them under uke's legs. Tori controls uke's upper body by holding uke's head with the right hand and trapping uke's right arm by passing the left arm under it. To secure the pin, tori pushes the hips into uke and tries to keep the heels together.

SCARF HOLD

For *kesagatame* tori sits next to uke with his or her head facing uke's head. Tori puts the right arm around uke's neck (like a scarf) and grabs the right knee, palm facing down. Tori secures uke's right arm by tucking it under the left armpit and grabbing hold of uke's sleeve with the left hand. For balance, tori spreads the legs apart wide and keeps the head down. Tori must maintain chest contact with the opponent to make it more difficult for the opponent to escape.

SHOULDER HOLD

Katagatame begins with uke lying on his or her back and tori kneeling on the right knee next to uke's right side. Tori places the left leg straight out to the left with the foot flat on the mat. Tori controls uke's upper body by pushing uke's right arm across uke's face and placing his or her head behind uke's arm. Tori then wraps the right arm around and under uke's head and clasps the hands together. To secure the pin, tori squeezes with the arms.

If you desire to have solid ne waza skills, then you should concentrate on learning *osaekomi waza* properly because it is the foundation for all other *ne waza* techniques. Without knowing how to control your opponent, keeping him or her on the ground, it will be impossible to execute any of the techniques covered in the next chapter on chokes and armlocks. Strong *osaekomi waza* will make your *tachi waza,* or standing techniques, better because it will give you the confidence to attempt more throws.

CHAPTER

8

CHOKES AND
JOINT LOCKS

hokes and joint locks are among the deadliest and devastating skills in judo. In competition, judoka use chokes to
constrict the neck. By restricting blood flow, chokes can
render a person unconscious in as little as five seconds. In self-
defense, chokes also attack the trachea and nerves in the neck,
potentially doing serious damage and even causing death.

In competition, judoka apply joint locks only to the elbow
because of the damage that they could cause to other limbs. Still,
it is possible for a joint lock to break the elbow. In judo self-defense,
the practitioner can attack all joints of the body. Joint locks are
capable of causing serious injury if applied with full power.

For success in both competition and self-defense, the judoka
should study chokes and joint locks thoroughly. The practitioner
should be able to enter these techniques from any throw or from
any ground situation.

CHOKES

The second branch of grappling skills that can be applied to randori are *shime waza*, choking techniques. In self-defense, shime are designed to attack any of the three areas of the neck. Some chokes attack the source of air by collapsing the trachea. Others cut off the blood flow so that the person will pass out from lack of oxygen in the brain. Finally, nerve chokes attack the nerves running through the neck. The result can be immobilization through pain or numbness. Many of the shime of judo attack more than one of these areas. Thus a judoka can literally choke a person by attacking nerves, arteries, and the trachea.

People who have not earned a black belt generally do not use choking techniques because they are extremely dangerous. A time limit is usually not imposed on chokes. Instead, the judoka holds the choke until the competitor taps out by patting the mat, partner, or self twice, or becomes unconscious. When applied properly, a choke can cause unconsciousness in just five seconds. If the practitioner releases shime immediately, harmful side effects generally do not occur. Although some feel that the only honorable reaction to an unbreakable choke is to resist it until unconsciousness occurs, the dangers associated with unconsciousness do not support this practice.

Although several methods of breaking choke holds are allowed in competition, the smart competitor will tap out if he or she cannot break the choke in seconds. Such an action is simply a measure of intelligence. It is better to lose a match than to risk serious, even potentially permanent, injury from being choked out.

Combat chokes attack the trachea, carotid arteries, and nerves in the neck. Competitive chokes are generally directed specifically against the carotid arteries. These chokes are thus safer because they do not take the chance of damaging the trachea or larynx.

Keep in mind that the judoka usually applies chokes when the opponent is on the mat after missing an attempted attack or when one's throw was unsuccessful in scoring a point but took the opponent down. In many cases the opponent will be attempting to rise and will be on all fours, on hands and knees. The person might also be in a sitting position in an attempt to rise or struggle. In either position, an experienced judoka can slip into a choke easily, locking it in place so it becomes immediately effective.

The main choking techniques taught in Kodokan judo are demonstrated in kneeling position to show actual positioning clearly.

TECHNIQUE TIPS FOR CHOKES

1. In choking techniques, precision is vitally important. The hands must be positioned very precisely and quickly, so be sure to study the details of each choke thoroughly.

2. The most opportune time to execute a choke is after an ineffective standing technique. Look for the opportunity during the transition from standing to ground fighting.

3. When applying any choke, keep the pressure continuous with your arms.

4. Employ your whole body in executing a choke. Use your legs to add strength to the choke or to hold your opponent in position while you are applying the choke.

5. Drill and practice choking techniques often without resistance until the actions become instinctual. The opportunity to choke in a live situation can be lost in seconds.

NAKED STRANGLE

Hadakajime is called the naked strangle because it is done with the bare arms, without using the jacket for leverage. Tori starts by kneeling behind uke. Tori takes the right arm and, with the palm facing down, passes it over uke's right shoulder and under uke's chin to the left side of uke's neck. With the left hand facing up, tori clasps the hands together near uke's left shoulder. Tori lowers his or her head and presses with the right side of the head against the left side of uke's head. Using the bony edge of the right forearm against uke's neck, tori pulls the hands toward himself or herself and into uke's throat, causing uke to submit.

SINGLE EDGE STRANGLE

For *katahajime* tori kneels behind uke. Tori takes the right hand and slides it from behind uke's right ear, passes it under uke's chin, and grabs uke's left lapel at about collarbone level. Tori passes the left hand under uke's left arm, lifts it toward himself or herself, and begins to pull the lapel with the right hand across uke's neck. To finish the choke, tori extends the left arm, passes it behind uke's head (and over the right forearm), and applies pressure to the back of uke's neck while continuing to pull the choke across uke's neck with the right-handed lapel grip.

SINGLE CROSS STRANGLE

Juji-jime, or cross strangle, is classified into three categories—
katajujijime (single cross strangle), *namijujijime* (normal cross
strangle), and *gyakujujijime* (reverse cross strangle). The three
chokes are distinguished by the different combinations in which
the hands are used. These chokes can be done from a variety of
different positions—on top of and astride the opponent, from
beneath, from beside, from behind, or even from the front in a
standing position.

The traditional way to perform katajujijime is by sitting on top
of the opponent in a straddle position. To begin, tori sits on top of
uke's abdominal region, straddling uke with a knee on the mat.
Tori takes the left hand and grabs uke's left lapel in a reverse grip
(thumb outside). With the right hand, tori grips uke's right lapel
in a normal way (fingers outside). To apply the strangle, tori pulls

a

with the left hand and presses slightly with the right hand, making sure to keep both hands against his or her chest. Tori applies pressure to both sides of uke's neck by crossing the hands to complete the strangle. For maximum efficiency one must be sure to have a deep grip with both hands.

NORMAL CROSS STRANGLE

Namijujijime, a slight variation of katajujijime, can also be done from several positions. Namijujijime, or normal cross strangle, is performed by taking a normal grip with both hands (i.e., both hands grip the gi with the thumb on the inside and the fingers outside). The following example of namijujijime is shown from a position in which tori is kneeling behind uke.

With uke sitting on the mat, tori kneels on the left knee immediately behind uke. Tori passes the left hand behind uke's neck and over uke's right shoulder to grab uke's left lapel, with the thumb inside. Tori reaches with the right hand over the left hand and arm and grabs the front part of uke's gi. Tori lowers his or her body over uke's left shoulder and applies the choke by pulling the hands together, crossing them behind uke's head. A slight variation of this technique is to apply the strangle while holding uke's upper body between the legs.

REVERSE CROSS STRANGLE

The most common way of applying *gyakujujijime* is from a bottom
position with tori facing uke and holding uke between the legs.
Tori starts by lying on his or her back with uke between the legs.
Tori reaches up with the left hand, and with the left palm facing
himself or herself (fingers inside), grabs uke's left collar deeply.
Tori passes the right hand over the left forearm and with the right
palm facing himself or herself (fingers inside) grabs uke's right
collar deeply. To apply the strangle, tori pulls both hands together
with arms crossed, applying pressure to both sides of uke's neck.
To prevent uke from standing up, tori pushes uke's knees away
with the feet. This choke can also be applied from the position
illustrated earlier in katajujijime.

TRIANGLE STRANGLE

Sankakujime is one of the most widely used choking techniques in international competition. Unlike the other shime waza techniques, sankakujime is done by using the legs to choke.

With uke on all fours (in a ball), tori grabs uke's belt with one hand and the back of uke's collar with the other. Tori drags uke toward himself or herself. Doing this will open uke up and create enough space to allow tori's legs to enter the starting position of the choke. Tori drops the right knee next to uke's head and places the left foot behind uke's opposite elbow. Tori tries to get the left foot to touch the right knee, forming a triangle with the legs. While squeezing the legs together, tori grabs uke's left arm with the right hand and rolls to the left, pulling uke along. As tori rolls, he or she straightens the left leg and forces the right leg on top of uke's body, making sure to capture uke's arm between the legs. Tori pulls uke's sleeve toward himself or herself with the right hand and places the left foot inside the right knee. To apply the choke, tori squeezes the legs together and does a hamstring curl with the right leg, pulling it toward himself or herself.

SLIDING LAPEL STRANGLE

For *okurierijime* tori starts by reaching with the right hand from below uke's right ear down along the neck and grabs uke's left lapel. After securing the lapel, tori starts to pull the choke to the right. The higher on the lapel tori grabs, the tighter the strangle will be. With the left hand, tori reaches under uke's left arm and grabs the far lapel (uke's right, in this case.) To execute the choke, tori continues to pull across uke's neck with the right hand while pulling directly downward with the left. Done properly, the choke will quickly result in a submission.

JOINT-LOCKING TECHNIQUES

The final branch of grappling skills used in competitive judo are joint locks. These are called *kansetsu waza*, literally meaning "joint techniques." Although in self-defense judo all the joints are examined from the perspective of manipulation, in contest judo these techniques are generally directed only against the elbow joint because it is least susceptible to accidental injury. Although a few joint locks work on the leg, they are illegal in modern competition, though still practiced for self-defense.

Kodokan judo permits two ways of locking the arm for randori or shiai. In the first method the elbow is locked out straight, using a part of the judoka's body to apply pressure against the joint to keep it locked out. In various arm locks the judoka uses the hips, armpit, knees, and hands to apply the locking pressure.

The second method is to wrap the arm in a bent position, cranking the arm to apply pressure on the shoulder. The body is controlled along with the arm. The judoka can generate the greatest control by pressure on the joint being manipulated.

When caught in a kansetsu waza, a judoka normally attempts an escape. Upon realizing that the hold cannot be broken, however, he or she should tap out. A kansetsu waza is extremely dangerous and can easily dislocate the elbow or shoulder, possibly resulting in permanent injury. It is wise to surrender before injury occurs.

The following kansetsu waza, joint locks, are commonly used in judo competition.

ARM HOLD

For *udegatame*, arm hold, tori traps uke's wrist against the shoulder. Tori places both hands outside uke's elbow and twists uke's elbow joint inward. Classic udegatame is usually executed from a loose kesagatame position. Tori sits beside uke in a modified kesagatame position with the left arm under uke's right arm. Uke will typically reach up with the right hand by tori's left ear to push tori away. As uke does this, tori traps uke's right wrist between the left shoulder and left side of the neck. Tori immediately applies the palm of the left hand to the back of uke's right elbow and places the right hand on top of the left. Tori extends uke's right arm by pulling away from uke a bit. With the left knee, tori kneels on uke's abdomen, limiting uke's mobility. Tori applies the arm lock by pressing against uke's right elbow with both hands, pulling the hands into himself or herself.

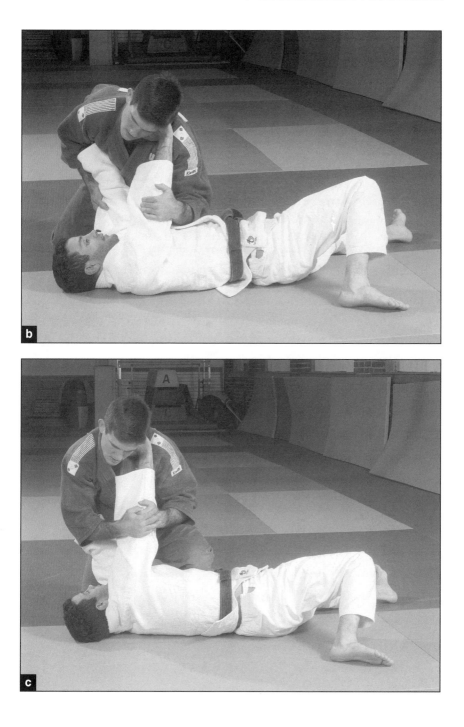

ARMPIT HOLD

Wakigatame can be done from a standing position as well as during ground fighting (ne waza). Tori holds one of uke's arms firmly under the armpit, stretches it out, and bends uke's elbow joint backward. Standing wakigatame is done when the opponent reaches out with one hand to grab the lapel.

The judoka can apply wakigatame in ne waza in a number of ways. The example illustrates wakigatame from the bottom position in ne waza. Tori starts by kneeling on all fours with uke to the rear. As uke reaches with the right hand over tori's back and under tori's right armpit to grab the sleeve, tori traps uke's right wrist under the right armpit. Tori drops the head and withdraws the body by circling away from uke and slipping from under uke's armpit. Tori swings the left leg over the right, sitting out backward and placing the body weight on the back of uke's right shoulder. With legs spread wide, tori applies the arm lock by straightening the body backward and pulling uke's right arm up with uke's elbow joint against tori's ribs.

CROSS HOLD

For *jujigatame* tori places both legs perpendicularly across uke's torso with one arm squeezed between the thighs. Holding uke's wrist with both hands, tori bends uke's elbow joint backward by pulling the wrist to the chest and arching the hips.

Jujigatame is one of the most popular arm locks used today in international competition. The many entries into this arm lock simply cannot be covered in this book. But the judoka should be familiar with how to execute and finish this move should the opportunity to do so ever arise.

With uke lying flat on the back, tori stands over uke and takes hold of one of uke's arms (the right in this example). With uke's arm straight, tori moves the right foot as close as possible to uke's body. Tori swings the left leg over uke's head and places it close to uke's left ear. At the same time, tori squats and then sits down as close to uke's right shoulder as possible, catching uke's outstretched arm between the legs. Tori lies on his or her back, simultaneously straightening uke's arm and squeezing the legs together.

To apply the arm lock, tori pulls the whole arm down toward the abdomen and chest. Tori makes sure that uke's wrist is turned so that uke's pinkie finger is closer to tori's chest (uke's thumb is up in the air). Usually this will do the trick; however, it may be necessary to increase leverage and pressure on uke's arm by lifting the hips off the mat and continuing to pull the arm toward the chest.

a

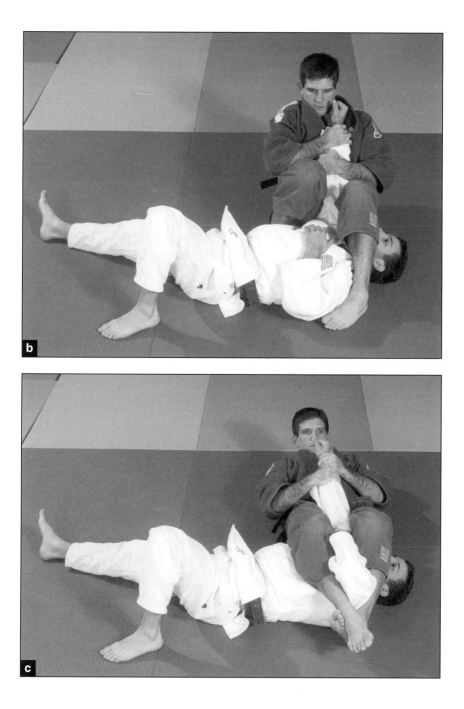

KNEE HOLD

For *hizagatame* tori holds uke's wrist under the armpit and presses it downward from the outside with the knee. Tori lies on the back with uke kneeling between the legs. Tori places both feet on uke's hips and pulls uke toward himself or herself by grabbing uke's right sleeve with the left hand (elbow high) and grabbing uke's left lapel with the right hand. Tori releases the left-handed grip and wraps the left arm around uke's right arm, trapping uke's right wrist under the left armpit.

Tori places the left palm on uke's right elbow and begins to apply pressure over uke's elbow joint. Simultaneously, tori makes uke lean forward by pushing the right foot against the inside of uke's left thigh. Tori controls uke by applying the left foot against the right side of uke's abdomen. To apply the arm lock, tori continues to push uke's right elbow with the left hand and adds pressure by using the left knee against uke's right elbow joint.

ARM WRAP

For *udegarami* tori grabs uke's wrist with one hand and with the other hand grasps his or her own wrist. Tori forces uke's elbow joint backward in a circular motion.

Unlike the other arm locks covered in this chapter that apply pressure to a straightened arm, udegarami applies pressure to the arm when it is in a bent L-shaped position. Like many judo grappling techniques, udegarami can be executed from several positions.

The most common application of udegarami is done from a yokoshihogatame-type position. Tori approaches uke from the right side, lying perpendicular to uke with chest on chest. Tori grips uke's left wrist with the left hand in such a way that the palm is holding the inner side of uke's wrist. Tori then slips the right hand under the upper part of uke's left arm and grasps his or her own left wrist with the knuckles pointing upward. To apply the arm lock, tori levers up uke's upper arm by raising the right elbow and shoulder and slightly pulling the right arm toward himself or herself.

a

Chokes and joint locks are two ways to end a competitive judo match with the score of ippon. In self-defense, they are perhaps the most effective means to subdue an attacker. For success in both competition and self-defense, the judoka should study chokes and joint locks thoroughly and be able to perform them from any throw or from any ground situation.

CHAPTER

9

COUNTERS AND COMBINATIONS

n judo, as in all martial arts, the practitioner must master basic moves before developing the advanced skills. Even after mastering the basic skills, however, the judoka must understand that many of the advanced abilities come from being able to change from one technique into another. This is an aspect of the flexible nature of ju. In the previous chapters you learned the basic throws, chokes, joint locks, and holds that are essential to good judo. In this chapter you will learn what it takes to counter an opponent who possesses the same knowledge and how to combine your skills into effective combinations. The key to successful sport judo is the flexibility to combine all your skills into one effective defense or attack.

COUNTERING TECHNIQUES

All judo competitors, no matter how accomplished, will be facing people of the same skill level. Even though they may have impeccable technique, their opponents will occasionally maneuver them into a position to be thrown or will put them in a pin, choke, or joint lock. The judoka must therefore be able to counter an opponent's technique. Countering techniques are known in judo as *kaeshi waza*.

Although a throw or a pin can cost a judoka a match, when the person has proper ukemi (breakfall) skills, injury will seldom occur. When it comes to chokes and joint locks, however, the possibility of serious injury is present. In using the counter that applies to chokes and joint locks, one should apply it in the first few seconds of resistance. If this is not possible, it is best to capitulate rather than be choked into unconsciousness or have an elbow dislocated or broken.

First, let us deal with the primary techniques of judo, the throws, which are divided into three standing categories and two sacrifice, or "falling," skills. Standing throws occur through the primary action of the hands, hips, or legs, although in all throws the whole body is used.

When an opponent begins to apply a throw, the judoka who has mastered the principle of ju can perceive the energy that will be required to make the throw work before the application of the technique. The judoka can therefore initiate a countering technique—a throw, pin, choke, or joint lock—before the opponent can break his or her balance.

This kind of ability takes much practice. More important, the judoka must also be uke (receiver) to many throws. There is no substitute for practice. Although learning to do a throw takes countless repetitions, learning to counter a throw effectively takes just as much time, if not more.

Acting as uke, the judoka feels the flow of energy being directed against him or her to break balance and allow the opponent to position for a throw. The judoka must counter the throw before the actual application of the kake. In truth, the counter begins either by not allowing balance to be broken or by directing the energy so that the loss of balance can be controlled and directed to the benefit of the defender.

This level of sensitivity is the mark of a superior martial artist. The judoka who wants the ability to apply and counter throws effectively should strive to attain it.

Once the judoka learns to sense the attacker's attempt to gain kuzushi, the superior martial artist will take control of the push or pull and blend with the tsukuri to counter throw, or otherwise counter, the opponent.

For example, suppose an opponent attempts ogoshi. As the person positions the body for the throw, the left shoulder, assuming a right-handed throw, must rotate back as the hips enter proper position for the throw. If the defender gently pushes on the shoulder as the competitor turns in, the defending judoka can take the opponent's balance and use a nidan kosotogari, two-level minor outer reaping throw, to win the point.

Again, the secret is having a high level of sensitivity so that one can sense the direction of energy the opponent is directing against him or her. Note that this sensitivity is an aspect of the principle of ju, which has become a lost art in many judo schools. Ju is what marks the difference between real judo as founded by Jigoro Kano, and pseudo judo, which has developed in modern times and is all too often founded on brute strength.

The greatest master of the past generation was Kyuzo Mifune, who lived from 1883 to 1965. Most people regard Mifune as the greatest master of the Kodokan in the period from 1938, when Kano died, until 1965, when Mifune died. Mifune taught that a judoka needed to be sensitive and aware to be successful in randori.

Mifune was one of the advocates of the theory of sphericity, the idea that human movement should be like the rolling of a ball. Mifune often placed a ball on the mats at the Kodokan and rolled it around to demonstrate how a ball rotates when pushed or pulled. He would then demonstrate that the judoka should move in the same way when acted upon by the push or pull of an opponent. Mifune described the principle of ju with the admonition to "enter when pulled, turn when pushed." Although that description is usually associated with aikido styles, it shows the original similarity of the two arts when they were based on the same jujutsu roots.

Sphericity is the key to kaeshi waza. Circular movements can thwart any throwing attempt. If the circular motion is continued, the opponent can easily be thrown with his or her own energy. Although the term *kaeshi* is translated as "counter," its literal meaning is "return" or "overturn." Thus the idea of a kaeshi waza is to return the strength the attacker is using for a throw back to the attacker in the form of a counter throw or other technique.

Note that kaeshi waza can be techniques other than throws. For example, if an opponent attempts an ippon seoinage, one-point shoulder throw, the defender can use a rolling motion of the right arm to slide the arm into a position to apply a hadakajime, naked strangle.

Kaeshi waza are excellent skills for defending against attempts of *tachi waza,* standing techniques, especially throws. But the other half of judo happens while lying on the mat. These are the ne waza, lying techniques, or katame waza, holding techniques.

As noted earlier, there are three divisions—pins (osae waza), chokes (shime waza), and joint locks (kansetsu waza). These excellent skills can render an opponent helpless in as little as 5 seconds. To score, the judoka must hold the pin for at least 10 seconds; to win a full point, the judoka must hold the pin for 25 seconds.

The current trend in judo emphasizes ground-fighting skills. Thus a judoka must know not only how to apply all mat techniques but also how to counter such skills. The essence of ground-fighting skills is still the principle of ju. The better one understands this concept, the more powerful one's skill, following the ancient saying, "In gentleness is strength."

Against these katame waza, holding techniques, the judoka uses fusegi, defenses, also called nogare waza, forms of escape. Every hold, whether a pin, choke, or joint lock, has a flow of movement and energy. Through the principle of ju a judoka can sense the flow of energy and move to defend or escape from the hold.

After an opponent has fully applied a pin, choke, or joint lock, the only thing that can happen if a judoka resists too long is injury. Although a player should never give up too easily, he or she should not risk a career-threatening injury.

Each hold, however, whether pin, choke, or joint technique, has a point before it is locked when the defender can escape without harm. The judoka must be able to recognize this moment through a high level of sensitivity, developed by being the uke to a fellow judoka practicing the holds. The more one feels the techniques applied, the more sensitive one becomes to the moment the hold is actually locked. The practitioner who can identify the moment just before the technique is locked can escape the hold and flow into a katame waza of his or her own.

One of the main methods taught to escape or defend against katame waza is the ability to anticipate the movement and prevent the moment of capture. The judoka creates a space to slip loose an arm to break a pin, extricate the neck from a choke, or bend or straighten the elbow to prevent a joint lock.

Some nogare waza involve the use of pushes or pulls to create a physical space through which the judoka can move to escape a pin, choke, or joint lock. The judoka can learn ways of sliding the entrapped arm to get it loose from the entrapment of a pin. Many chokes can be countered by pushing or pulling on the elbow of the arm pressing the forearm against the neck. Finally, there are ways of pushing or pulling with the arm being held in a joint lock.

One of the most important characteristics of a good judoka is flexibility. The more flexible the practitioner, the greater the chance of escape from any hold. Many people do not realize how important flexibility is to the judoka. Some focus exclusively on strength. Although it is important to be strong, it is just as important to use the principle of ju, which includes not only yielding to force but also being flexible in response and body.

Another aspect of improved flexibility is the ability to use the legs. In many pins, the opponent holds at least one arm and the upper torso helpless. With one free hand, the defender can only do so much. Yet with proper flexibility in the spine and legs, especially in the hip joints, it is possible to use the legs with the same dexterity as one uses the arms.

With this added ability, one can overcome many holds that were previously unbreakable. The legs and feet can be used to hook the head, arms, and legs of an opponent attempting an osae waza, pinning technique. Once the person catches any of these limbs, he or she can use the legs to create a space for the arm or torso to move and extricate itself from the hold. The judoka can then use the legs in application of certain holds such as sankakujime, the triangle choke, formed by the legs, or jujigatame, the cross lock, in which the legs hold the upper body immobile while the arm is locked by a pull of the hands on the wrist, with the hips pushing upward on the elbow.

A person can excel in judo only by mastering the individual skills of nage waza, osae waza, shime waza, and kansetsu waza. The last three divisions are known as katame waza or ne waza. Yet it is not enough to master the tachi waza of standing techniques or the ne waza of ground fighting.

A true expert of Kodokan judo must also know how to counter every technique in the judo repertoire. He or she must be able to counter nage waza through the medium of kaeshi waza and counter katame waza through nogare kata and fusegi. One develops this ability through practice of the primary techniques as both tori and uke and consistent practice in the countering skills themselves.

But one must never forget that all countering skills in judo are based on the principle of ju. When Jigoro Kano created Kodokan judo, he did so with the idea of basing all the skills, movements, and countermoves on the principle of yielding and flexibility. Judo is the art of combat based on the principle of ju, in which the skill of being soft, gentle, and pliant overcomes the strength and aggressiveness of any opponent. This is the art of judo; this is the way of counter techniques.

Competitive judo is an art unto itself. Although Kano developed randori from the ranotoru he learned from his Kito Ryu jujutsu instructors and then developed shiai, or contest, judo from the practice of randori, he always wanted the sport to be within the context of the art of judo.

After Kano's death in 1938, competitive judo developed until it was accepted as an Olympic sport in 1964. Since then the Kodokan has developed along mainly competitive lines, so that the face of judo has completely changed since its origins.

Along with competition, Kano created an excellent art of self-defense. From 1884 until the late 1950s and for a short while in the early 1960s, Kodokan judo was known as an effective method of combat. Some older practitioners of judo remember the days of self-defense training and continue to practice this aspect of the martial art.

Most judo practitioners today, however, focus on the sport of judo, with an eye toward Olympic competition. Yet to be successful in Olympic judo, one must have complete knowledge of judo and a strategic method of applying the skills of randori.

The judoka must be competent with skills on both the left and right sides, yet the standard idea these days is to develop a tokui waza, favorite technique, to an almost unstoppable level on one side. One must have both strong offensive skills and solid defensive skills.

In the development of defensive skills, the judoka must gain understanding of all kaeshi waza, nogare kata, and fusegi. Through these skills, the practitioner can counter any throw, pin, choke, or joint lock.

In the improvement of offense, the judoka must practice each of the individual techniques themselves. Many of the old masters would use only one throw to win in randori. Their skills were so magnificent that they could move about in a randori, shift into a technique, and throw the opponent cleanly for a full point score (ippon).

Many of the great masters, such as Kyuzo Mifune and Sakujiro Yokoyama, often won their matches with throws, never bothering to go to the mat and never needing to because of their great skill. Yet it is possible to develop ground skills so effective that once a katame waza is applied, the match is won without worry.

NIDAN KOSOTOGARE

Nidan kosotogare is a rear counter technique which is typically used against forward techniques like ogoshi and haraigoshi. In this example, uke attempts ogoshi (to the right). Tori gives resistance by pushing on uke's right shoulder with the left hand and pulls uke's right hand back toward him or her. As uke begins to turn his or her back, tori continues to push on uke's shoulder, reaping the back of the support leg (left) with his or her left leg. Tori also pushes uke's left arm into the abdomen using his or her right hand. Tori uses the right leg both for support and as a driving leg.

IPPON SEIONAGE TO BRITISH STRANGLE

On many occasions the most opportune moment to catch an opponent in ne waza is during the transition from tachi waza to newaza. This is a perfect example. As uke enters into drop seionage (to the right), tori steps to the right to avoid the attack. Once the momentum of the attempted throw has been stopped, tori quickly slides his or her right hand under the opponent's chin (typically tori's right hand will already be holding the opponent's lapel). Next, tori steps over uke's back with the left leg, sliding it between the opponent's abdomen and the mat. With his or her left hand tori grabs the outside of the opponent's left knee and somersaults to turn the opponent on his back. To secure the choke, tori pulls uke's knee toward him with the left hand and tightens the choke with his or her right hand by pulling hard and circling toward the opponent's legs with his body.

a

(continued)

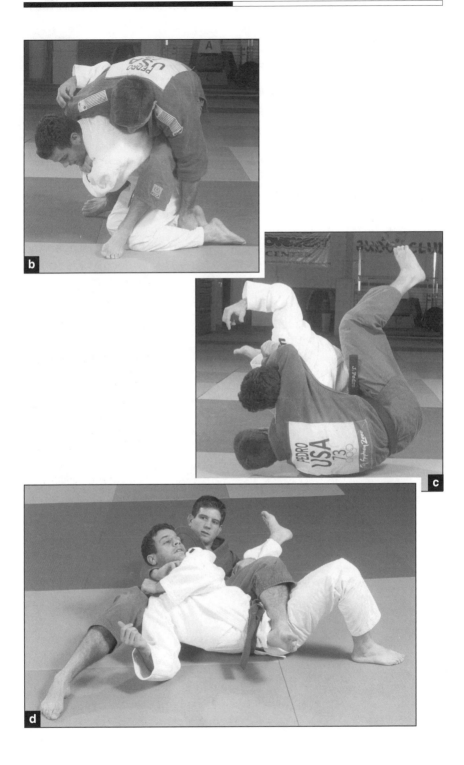

TECHNIQUE TIPS FOR IPPON SEIONAGE TO BRITISH STRANGLE

1. Make sure that you have stopped the momentum of the attack before jumping on the opponent's back.
2. Do not hesitate as the critical moment for success disappears quickly (do not give the opponent a chance to cover up).
3. Practice transition techniques (tachi waza to ne waza) often to improve reaction time.

CONTINUOUS TECHNIQUES

The first goal of the judoka is to perfect the individual throws, pins, chokes, and joint locks. Once the person has developed these to the highest level through mastery of kuzushi (balance breaking), tsukuri (body positioning), and kake (application of the technique), he or she must learn to go beyond doing one movement at a time.

Contest judo is essentially a method of applying the principle of ju in competition. Applying a throw, a pin, a choke, or even a joint lock requires the use of ju, exhibited through balance breaking made possible by yielding to a push or pull, or by eliciting a reaction to one's own push or pull.

All other facets, including the two advanced strategies to be covered here, are outgrowths of kuzushi, tsukuri, and kake applied through the concept of ju.

After mastering each individual technique, the judoka must become capable of applying them in continuous fashion. When competing against a proficient and experienced opponent, a throw may fail because of the opponent's superior balance. When that happens, a judoka can attempt to continue the process of kuzushi while trying the same throw again. This is called *renzoku waza*. A skilled judoka will usually attempt a throw no more than three times. If the judoka feels the opponent losing balance, however, he or she may make another attempt. Stories are told of famous judoka who would dive in with an attack, using a throw such as ogoshi to weaken the balance and position of the opponent. The judoka might make a second attempt and then a third before finally overwhelming the opponent and throwing him to the mat. The first or second throwing attempt often breaks the balance so that a subsequent attempt is successful. But one should realize that if the opponent is perfectly balanced on the first attempt, it would not be wise to use the same technique again because the balanced individual is capable of performing a throw or hold of his or her own.

Renzoku waza, continuous techniques, are an important part of competitive judo. Continuous techniques should be practiced and developed to a high degree. Like all judo skills, renzoku waza is based on the principle of ju and begins with breaking the opponent's balance. A judoka can apply renzoku waza only after disrupting an opponent's balance.

COMBINATION TECHNIQUES

Another skill that the judoka should develop, a skill possibly more important then renzoku waza, is *renraku waza*, which means "combination technique," or "connection technique." Renraku waza is the concept of combining techniques so that the judoka can flow smoothly from one technique into another one, and still another. If one technique fails, the judoka simply continues to another, and perhaps yet others, until the opponent is down. The ability to combine techniques is important because it offers the judoka another strategy. If a throw fails to take an opponent down, it is because the opponent has made a movement of resistance. This movement of resistance closes the opportunity for the original throw. If balance is disrupted, however, the judoka applies renzoku waza. If the opponent maintains balance, renraku waza becomes the logical choice.

For example, suppose a judoka first attempts an ouchigari, major inner reaping throw, and it does not work. This throw generally fails because the opponent has countered the kuzushi directed to the back and countered the throwing motion against the left leg. The judoka could move the right leg from where it was hooking the opponent's left leg and bring it across the opponent's right leg, throwing the opponent in a taiotoshi, body drop. Everything being the same, an alternative finishing throw could be a haraigoshi, sweeping hip throw.

Another aspect of renraku waza is that the judoka can follow up a throw that has caused the opponent to fall but lacks the form to gain a scoring point. At this juncture, the judoka can follow the opponent down and move right into a pin or other grappling technique. For example, if a judoka tries an osotogari, major outer reaping throw, but does not score with it, he or she can easily follow the opponent down and apply kesagatame or katagatame.

It is also possible to go into a standing choke or joint lock from an attempted throw. For example, the judoka might attempt a kouchigari, minor inner reaping, or ouchigari, major inner reaping. Finding it impossible to throw the opponent backward, the judoka could then switch the hands into a katajujijime, single cross choke.

The potential renraku waza, including the many variations that can be created from the basic techniques, are endless. A judoka who can apply a series of techniques can adapt to any situation. Renraku waza can be skills that go from throws to other throws, to pins, to chokes, or to joint locks. They can be combinations of pins to other pins, to chokes, or to joint locks. Or they can be other combinations.

TECHNIQUE TIPS FOR COMBINATIONS

Many varieties of combination attacks can be used in judo, and the number of possible combination techniques is endless. A judoka who desires to be successful should be able to perform all of the types of combinations listed here. As a rule, the more unpredictable you can make your attacks, the better. Remember to use ashi waza, or foot techniques, to set up your major throws.

1. Faking a throw. In this combination, faking one throw will create a reaction by your opponent that will enable you to enter into a main throw. The key is to make the initial feint a real threat.

2. Continuous attacks. In this combination, you attempt to throw your opponent with one throw and, if unsuccessful, attack with another throw before your opponent has a chance to recover fully.

3. Complementing throws. In this combination, having multiple throws that complement one another (front and back) from the same grip will keep your opponent guessing about which attack you will make.

OUCHIGARI TO TAIOTOSHI

Ouchigari to taiotoshi is a classic example of a combination technique. This combination begins when tori makes a strong ouchigari (right) attack that uke stops and defends by lifting and stepping back with the left leg. Uke's left foot will touch the mat and, as he or she recovers, uke's momentum will begin to come forward. Tori then steps down with the right foot and begins taiotoshi by pulling uke's left hand and stepping around with the left leg. To finish, tori brings his or her right leg across and in front of uke's right leg.

OSOTOGARI TO KESAGATAME

Osotogari to kesagatame is an example of a combination technique made up of a natural continuation of events. After throwing uke with osotogari (left), tori should still be holding the opponent's sleeve with his right hand. Tori then follows opponent to the ground into newaza by landing next to uke's body. Tori secures uke's left arm by placing uke's left hand under his or her own right armpit. Tori gains control of the opponent's head and finishes the pin by bringing the left arm around and under uke's head. It's important for tori to keep the legs spread apart for balance and to keep the head down. Once again, the key to success lies in the quickness to make the transition from tachiwaza to newaza.

Competitive success comes from complete knowledge of individual techniques that can be applied fully and powerfully to score. But for dealing with a skillful, competent opponent, the secrets to success are kaeshi waza, renzoku waza, and renraku waza.

CHAPTER
10

COMPETITION

In many parts of the world, competitions are held regularly at the local developmental level on up to the elite international level. Jigoro Kano did not want competitions to be only about winning. Their purpose is not only to determine champions. Rather, competitions are an excellent way to evaluate one's progress in judo and provide a competitive training ground that supplements regular practice sessions. Of course, everyone likes to win, but you should view competition as an opportunity to test your skills against others to determine your strengths and weaknesses.

Through competition you can learn valuable lessons. During competitions, try to make your favorite techniques work without making any mistakes. As you more frequently perform mistake-free techniques, you know that your techniques are becoming stronger. Conversely, if you are consistently getting beat in a particular area, you know that you need to concentrate more on that area during practice. Through participation in regular competitions, you will increase your technical development tremendously and will get a true understanding of your proficiency.

By approaching competitions in this way, you will raise your level of mental, spiritual, and physical development. After all, the winner may not be the one who won the contest today, but the one who learns, makes corrections, improves, and gives more effort to becoming a better judoka tomorrow.

Besides providing competition, tournaments offer opportunities to become involved and make a difference in your judo community. Adult judo players often volunteer their time as referees and officials at tournaments. Other judo students and parents participate as volunteer scorers, timekeepers, match recorders, and tournament staff. Each of these jobs requires technical knowledge, dedication, and sacrifice, and helps contribute to the success of the event.

COMPETITION BASICS

Individual judo competitions are held regularly on the local, state, national, and international levels. Local, state, and national judo competitions are generally separated into gender, age, and weight categories. Some competitions even use separate divisions according to rank. Tournaments use single, double, and repechage elimination systems. All international events, including the Olympic Games, separate divisions only according to gender and weight—seven categories for men and seven for women (see table 10.1)—and use a European double repechage elimination system.

Although held only occasionally in the United States, team competitions are popular events elsewhere in the world. Team

TABLE 10.1
Judo Weight Classifications

Class	Men	Women
Bantamweight	Under 60 kg	Under 48 kg
Featherweight	Under 66 kg	Under 52 kg
Lightweight	Under 73 kg	Under 57 kg
Light middleweight	Under 81 kg	Under 63 kg
Middleweight	Under 90 kg	Under 70 kg
Light heavyweight	Under 100 kg	Under 78 kg
Heavyweight	Over 100 kg	Over 78 kg

Some competitions have an open weight category.

judo matches consist exclusively of male or female teams, with five to seven persons per team.

REGISTRATION AND WEIGH-IN

Before being allowed to compete, an athlete must register for the event. Registration typically involves showing some sort of identification, proof of age, and a current judo membership card on the day of competition. Because all competitions are separated according to weight, each competitor weighs in so that the divisions can be made. Following the weigh-in, most events pair contestants randomly to determine who will compete against whom.

COMPETITION AREA

A judo competition takes place inside a large square marked on the *tatami,* or mat. The competition area includes two zones (contest zone and danger zone) and must be at least 8 meters by 8 meters (maximum of 10 meters by 10 meters). The danger zone, typically red, is 1 meter wide. Outside the competition area, a 3-meter safety area is added for protection (figure 10.1).

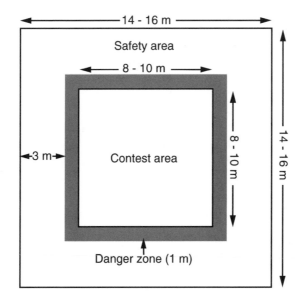

Figure 10.1   The dimensions and features of a judo competition area.
Reprinted, by permission, from Human Kinetics, 1998, The sports rule book, (Champaign, IL: Author), 171.

At the start of a match, competitors are required to bow before entering the competition area. Each player then walks to a taped line on the mat, bows to the opponent, and takes one step forward to signify readiness to compete. When both contestants are ready, the referee will begin the match by saying, "Hajime!" If a competitor accidentally steps outside the danger zone during the match, the referee assesses a penalty. If one or both competitors go outside the competition area during the action, the referee stops the contest and applies no penalty. If a competitor stays in the danger zone for five seconds without making an attack, penalty points are given. At the conclusion of the match, the players return to their respective lines, await the decision, and bow to each other. They also bow before exiting the competition area.

UNIFORM

Competitors must wear clean judo gis, either blue or white. The competitor whose name appears first in the bracket sheet wears blue, and his or her opponent wears white. In some local and regional events, both contestants wear white uniforms, with the first competitor called wearing a red or blue sash. The referee and judges can thus distinguish between contestants in the confusion of the action and score the contest properly.

Boys and men are not allowed to wear anything under the jacket, but females must wear a plain white T-shirt under the jacket. Competitors must have clean, short fingernails. Long hair must be worn up or in a ponytail held by an elastic band or scrunchie. Competitors cannot wear rings, earrings, metal, or other potentially harmful objects. Contestants may not wear glasses but may wear soft contact lenses at their own risk.

Referees strictly observe the size and width of judo uniforms to ensure fairness of competition. The contestant is responsible for being sure that the uniform meets those standards. Otherwise, he or she may be asked to change into one that fits properly.

OFFICIALS

A judo match is judged by three officials (one referee and two line judges). The referee conducts the match, awards all penalties and scores, and announces the outcome of the match. It is the referee's responsibility to ensure that the scores are recorded properly and

The referee awards an ippon.

that the contest is fought according to the rules. The referee is free to move about the mat area, shadowing the competitors, to get the best angle to view the contest. Common referee commands are shown in table 10.2.

The two judges sit at opposite corners outside the contest area and assist the referee in making calls. When a judge's opinion differs from the score or penalty announced by the referee, the judge is obliged to so indicate by making the appropriate official gesture. When both judges agree to a score different from the one announced by the referee, they overrule the referee. When all three officials signal different scores, the referee announces the middle value score.

TABLE 10.2
Common Referee Commands and Gestures

Commands

Hajime	"Begin." Start fighting.
Matte	"Stop." The referee holds an arm straight out with the palm facing the scorer's and timer's table.
Soremade	"That is all." (Indicates the end of the match.)
Osaekomi	"Hold down." Signifies that a pin has been secured. The referee holds an arm out in front and over the pin at a 45 degree angle, palm facing down.
Toketa	"Escape." Indicates that the hold down has been broken. The referee waves an arm (straightened) back and forth over the competitors.
Sonomama	"Freeze." Usually called during osaekomi to award a penalty.
Yoshi	"Continue." Called by the referee after a sonomama.
Hantei	"Judgment." The referee holds the colored flag of the contestant he or she believes won the match above the head. The judges do the same, and the match is awarded to the contestant who receives a majority vote.
Hikiwake	"Draw." The referee extends an arm in front halfway between the contestants (used only in team competition).

Gestures

Award ippon	The referee raises one arm high above the head with the palm of the hand facing forward.
Award waza-ari	The referee raises one arm, sideways, to shoulder height with the palm facing downward.
Award waza-ari-awasete-ippon	Referee performs waza-ari gesture, then ippon gesture.

Award yuko	The referee raises one arm to 45 degrees from the body with the palm facing downward.
Award koka	The referee raises one arm bent at the elbow with the thumb toward the shoulder and the palm facing forward.
Penalty (shido, chui, keikoku)	The referee points at the contestant with the index finger extended from a closed fist.
Noncombativity	The referee rotates the arms in a forward motion at chest height and then points at the contestant with the forefinger.
Adjustment of judo gi	The referee crosses the left hand over the right, palms facing inward, at belt height.
Cancellation of an expressed opinion	The referee repeats the cancelled gesture while raising the other hand above the head to the front and waving it from right to left two or three times.

CONDUCTING THE MATCH

The duration of a judo match is between three and five minutes of actual fighting time. The contest time for junior matches is three minutes. Senior women's matches are four minutes in length, and all senior men's matches are five minutes long.

During the match the referee may stop the contest for a number of reasons by calling, "Matte." In all such instances the competition clock is stopped.

The referee will stop a match when

- a contestant goes out of bounds,
- a contestant breaks the rules of the match or a penalty occurs,
- one contestant lifts the other off the mat during ground work,
- a stalemate occurs in ground work,
- confusion occurs,
- a contestant is injured and requests medical attention, or
- time runs out.

SCORING

During a judo competition, the object is to score an ippon, or one point (see table 10.3). When ippon is scored, the match is over. Judo players under age 13 can score an ippon in two ways—by throwing the opponent directly on to the back with speed and reasonable force or by pinning the opponent using a recognized hold down for 25 seconds. Players 13 and older can also score an ippon by strangling or choking the opponent until the opponent submits by tapping out. Players 17 and older can score an ippon in a fourth way by arm locking the opponent until submission.

If neither player achieves ippon during the match, the player with the highest single score wins. In judo, unlike most other sports, individual scores are not added together. Therefore, for example, a player with 1 *yuko* would beat an opponent who has 10 *kokas*. The only exception to this rule is the score of *waza-ari*. Two *waza-ari* scores add up to ippon.

TABLE 10.3
Scores

Score	Ways to Achieve
Ippon	1. Throw opponent with control largely on the back with considerable force and speed.
	2. Pin opponent for 25 seconds.
	3. Strangle or arm lock opponent into submission.
	4. Score two waza-aris.
Waza-ari	1. Throw opponent with control but technique lacks one of the three elements necessary for ippon (largely on back, speed, force).
	2. Pin opponent for 20 to 24 seconds.
Yuko	1. Throw opponent on the side.
	2. Pin opponent for 15 to 19 seconds.
Koka	1. Throw opponent onto the shoulder, thigh, or buttocks.
	2. Pin opponent for 10 to 14 seconds.

If neither player scores any points or if the match ends in a tie, the referee calls for a *hantei* (vote for decision). The referee and judges vote for a winner by raising the colored flag of that contestant (blue or white), and the referee awards the match to the winner.

PENALTIES

When a competitor breaks a rule, the referee awards a penalty. Penalties play a significant role in a judo competition. Penalties earn points, but not the kind a competitor wants because the penalty points are awarded to the opponent. To avoid getting penalties during a match, one must understand the rules. A smart judoka knows how to use the rules to his or her advantage and can win a match on penalties alone. Penalties range from minor infractions to disqualification. Unlike the normal scores for throwing and hold-downs, penalty points add up to the next highest score. The following is a list of the most common penalties and an explanation of when they are awarded.

> **Shido:** A *shido,* or note, the smallest infraction of the rules, is given for minor offenses. If a competitor receives a shido for any of the following offenses, the opponent will be awarded a koka.
>
> * Stalling or noncombativity
> * False attack
> * Adopting an extremely defensive posture
> * Standing in the danger zone without attacking (five seconds)
> * Grabbing inside opponent's sleeve or pants leg
> * Holding both hands on same side of gi (five seconds)
>
> **Chui:** A *chui,* or caution, is a more serious offense. If a contestant receives a penalty of chui for any of the following offenses, the opponent will be awarded a yuko.
>
> * Any combination of two shido penalties
> * Stepping out of the mat area on purpose
> * Crawling out of the mat area on purpose
> * Pushing the opponent out of the mat area
> * Kicking a hand or arm to make the opponent release his or her grip

Keikoku: A *keikoku,* or warning, is a severe penalty that is usually given for an offense judged to be dangerous. If a contestant receives a penalty of keikoku for any of the following offenses, the opponent will be awarded a waza-ari.

- Any combination of three shido penalties
- A chui and a shido penalty
- Unsporting conduct such as punching, kicking, biting, or swearing
- Performing any throw or hold judged to be dangerous to either competitor

Hansoku maki: *Hansoku maki,* or disqualification, is the severest penalty. A contestant who receives this penalty automatically loses the match because the opponent is awarded an ippon. In some instances, the disqualified player may not be able to compete again in the tournament. Any of the following results in hansoku maki.

- Any combination of two keikoku penalties
- Any combination of four penalties
- Execution of any technique that is illegal in the sport

ENDING THE MATCH

The match is over when a contestant scores an ippon or time expires. The referee will say, *"Soremade,"* meaning "that is all." Both contestants must immediately stop, return to their respective lines in the center of the mat, and wait for the decision from the referee. In the meantime, the contestants are required to fix their uniforms properly and tie their belts. The referee will indicate the winner by raising an arm toward the contestant who has won the match. The contestants then take one step backward and bow to one another. It has become common courtesy to shake hands as well (although this is not required). Before exiting the mat area, the contestants are required to bow at the edge of the mat.

It is important that the serious judoka be familiar with the elements that go into a judo match. It is just as important to prepare oneself away from the mat. Look to the next chapter on conditioning to learn the ways in which a judoka prepares himself or herself for the practice of the art.

CHAPTER

11

CONDITIONING

Training off the mat with activities like weightlifting and running is an excellent way to prepare the body physically for the sport of judo, strengthen the muscles, and help prevent injuries. Other circumstances may make it necessary to incorporate training methods outside the dojo. The serious competitor may find local club randori sessions inadequate to improve and achieve greatness because experienced opposition is not available. If time and distance prohibit training with more and better people, the ambitious judoka will have to train with methods like weightlifting and running. Another reason one may choose to train outside the dojo is to counter mental and physical staleness. An athlete who practices judo every day of the week for years on end can become bored. This boredom can increase the risk of injury. The recreational judo player who trains in twice-weekly randori sessions may not need any additional training, but the additional work certainly will not hurt.

In judo, as with most other forms of training, the judoka must consider two principles—progressive overload and specificity. The concept of progressive overload means that to improve, the individual must perform the chosen activity faster, longer, more frequently, or against more resistance than before. Although it is nearly impossible to achieve day-to-day improvements, the person should see improvement in one form or another every week or every month. One way to accomplish this is to keep records of the weights lifted or times ran. One must continually strive to lift more or run faster.

Specificity means training specifically for judo. In other words, off-mat training should be designed to help improve performance on the judo mat. The sport of judo requires muscular and cardio-vascular endurance, strength, flexibility, agility, and speed. The person who develops ability in all these areas will become a better judoka. Being able to bench 300 pounds and squat 400 pounds once does not necessarily help in judo, especially if the person cannot last longer than 30 seconds during randori. But the ability to sustain that strength for the entire length of the match or randori session would be valuable. Knowing what qualities one needs to improve will determine the most beneficial type of off-mat training.

WARM-UP AND COOL-DOWN

Physical preparation begins with the *taiso*, or body-manipulation exercises. These exercises are of two types—*junbi undo* and *shumatsu undo*, warm-up exercises and cool-down exercises, respectively. Junbi undo stretch, strengthen, and warm up the body. Some judo schools use a specific set of junbi undo to warm up before every class. Other schools use different sets of warm-ups to provide variety in training as well as to prepare the body for specific workouts, such as throwing or ground work.

WARM-UP

The judoka must warm up the body to prepare it for performing the skills of judo. A proper warm-up is the best way to prevent injury in the practice of any sport, especially one like judo that involves combat skill and close-quarter fighting.

Judo taiso encompasses three aspects. The first is the stretching of the muscles, tendons, and ligaments. In many ways this is the most important aspect of the taiso because muscles that are warm and stretched are much less likely to become injured.

TECHNIQUE TIPS FOR WARM-UP EXERCISES

1. Preworkout stretching should consist of active and dynamic exercises to prepare your body for the work that you will ask it to perform.

2. Begin by jogging lightly or skipping for approximately five minutes to get the blood flowing through your body before starting warm-up exercises.

3. Stretching is a slow and gradual process. Begin each exercise slowly and gradually increase the tempo of the movement to loosen up, but never bounce because doing so can cause injury.

4. Stretch as far as you comfortably can. If you have pain or feel tearing of any kind, stop exercising and avoid motions that may further aggravate the injury.

5. Breathe during the exercises, exhaling from the start to the full range of the stretch or motion.

6. When performing the strength exercises (e.g., sit-ups and push-ups), gradually increase the number of repetitions from week to week to increase strength.

The taiso should be vigorous enough to warm the body without wasting energy. People who wear themselves out getting ready to practice judo hinder their ability to learn the art.

The second aspect of judo taiso is strength building. Over time, strength exercises, specifically push-ups, leg raises, sit-ups, bridges, and others, gently and methodically build up the strength of the judoka. As the body becomes stronger, the person will find practicing the skills of judo easier. An inner strength develops that not only improves the performance of the muscles but also adds an extra aspect of coordination.

This quality, coordination, is the third aspect. Through the practice of the exercises, the body starts to develop greater coordination. Then, as the judoka practices the skills of judo, the body develops coordination to a much higher level.

Coordination has always been considered one of the most important aspects of martial-arts training. In Oriental philosophy, true strength comes from coordination between the mind and body. By using intense mental focus, a person can draw upon the full strength reserves of the human body.

The following is a basic, though incomplete, list of junbi undo or warm-up exercises.

NECK ROLLS

Bend your neck and then slowly roll your head a few times in each direction.

ARM SWINGS

Twist by swinging your arms from side to side in both directions a few times, rotating at the waist.

ARM CIRCLES

Swing your arms a few times in a big circle, first toward the ceiling and then toward the floor.

SIDE STRADDLES

Squat over one leg and put the other leg, foot flat on the floor, out to the side. Flex your outer thigh for 3 to 5 seconds. Relax, then stretch your inner thigh until it feels taut. Hold the stretch for 8 to 10 seconds. Repeat with the other leg.

FRONT, BACK, AND SIDE BENDS

Standing with your feet double shoulder-width apart, bend forward as far as you can and bring your hands through your legs. Hold the position for 8 to 10 seconds. Relax and reach back with your arms as far as possible, pushing your hips forward. Hold for 8 to 10 seconds. Next, place one hand on your hip and bend to the side reaching one arm over your head to the side you are bending. Hold for 8 to 10 seconds and repeat to the other side.

TRUNK TWISTS

Stand with your feet double shoulder-width apart. Bending at the waist, make a full circle with your upper body by starting over your right leg, continuing to the middle, then to your left and back upright again. Reverse directions and repeat a few times.

QUADRICEPS STRETCH

Standing with your feet shoulder-width apart, bend one leg, bringing the heel to your buttocks, and grab your ankle with your hand. Stretch the quadriceps muscle by pushing your hip forward and hold it for 3 to 5 seconds. Release the ankle and switch to the other leg. Repeat 5 times on each leg.

BUTTERFLY STRETCH

Sit on the floor and bring your feet as close to your groin as possible, keeping the bottoms of your feet together. Grab your feet and push your knees to the floor with your elbows. Hold for 8 to 10 seconds.

JUDO PUSH-UPS

From a modified push-up position (inverted v-shape) with the arms straight and feet double-shoulder width apart, bring your upper body toward the mat in a pendulum-like motion by bending your arms and lowering your chest and hips toward the mat. As your upper body passes, your arms straighten, pushing your upper body away from the mat. Only your feet and hands should be in contact with the mat throughout the duration of the exercise. Return to the starting position and perform 10 to 15 repetitions.

NECK BRIDGES

Support all of your weight either on your forehead (front) or back of your head (back) and your feet. While in a bridge, keep your hands off the mat and move forward and backward on your head slowly.

UKEMI

Do 8 to 10 repetitions of all ukemi exercises to loosen up your entire body and prepare it for judo practice.

JUMP OVERS

Stand next to your partner, who is tucked into a ball on his elbows and knees. Jump up and over your partner's back to the other side. As soon as your feet touch the floor, immediately hop back over your partner in the other direction. Repeat 10 to 15 times. This helps to create explosive quickness.

SQUAT THRUST

Start in a standing position and squat down by bending your legs. Place your hands on the mat in front of you. Keeping your hands on the mat, kick your legs back, straightening your body into an extended push-up position. Bring your legs back to your chest, into a tuck position, and then jump up into the air as high as you can. Repeat 10 to 15 times. This will help develop leg strength and explosiveness.

EBI

Lying on your left side with your feet straight, reach up with your arms. Dig your left elbow into the mat. Curl and bring your legs up to your elbow. Roll over your back to the right side and repeat the steps. Continue the exercise until you have gone down the entire length of the mat.

COOL-DOWN

Shumatsu undo are cool-down exercises that help the judoka maintain flexibility developed during the session and carry away the lactic acid accumulated during practice through the stretching and increased blood flow of the exercises. The cool-down can reduce soreness and promote quicker recovery from a grueling training session. Pages 164 to 169 show a few of the exercises that are used for shumatsu undo, cool-down.

TECHNIQUE TIPS FOR COOL-DOWN EXERCISES

1. Postworkout stretching should consist of slow, controlled movements aimed at lengthening the muscles.

2. Perform stretches slowly and gradually and stretch only as far as you comfortably can.

3. Hold each stretch for approximately 10 seconds. Rest and do the movement a second time, going a bit farther to begin to lengthen the stretch.

4. Relax during stretching and remember to exhale through the entire range of motion of the stretch.

5. Signs of overstretching include tearing, searing, or an electric sensation. If symptoms arise, stop stretching immediately.

ALTERNATING LOWER-BACK STRETCH

Lie on your back and bring your right leg across your body to the floor. Press your knee to the floor with your hand while keeping your shoulders in contact with the mat. Hold for 8 to 10 seconds and repeat to the left side.

SHOULDER STRETCH

Sitting on the mat, cross one arm in front of your chest and use
your other arm to pull it into your body to stretch your shoulder.
Hold for 8 to 10 seconds and repeat on the other side.

FRONT AND SIDE SPLIT STRETCH

Spread your legs apart as far as possible, keeping your toes up. Flex your thighs and hips for 3 to 5 seconds. Relax. Slowly bring your chest over your right knee until you feel tension and hold for 8 to 10 seconds. Relax, and then slowly bring your chest toward the floor. When you feel tension, hold for 8 to 10 seconds. Relax and then slowly bring your chest over your left knee until you feel tension and hold for 8 to 10 seconds. Repeat exercise 2 to 3 times.

TRICEPS STRETCH

Sitting on the mat, reach one arm behind your head trying to touch your opposite shoulder. Grab your elbow with your other hand and pull to stretch your triceps muscle. Hold for 8 to 10 seconds and repeat on the other side.

BEND AND EXTEND STRETCH

Standing with feet shoulder-width apart, bend, and grasp your ankles. Hold for up to 20 seconds. Relax and then extend by reaching your arms up over your head as high as you can and hold for 10 seconds. Repeat the exercise 2 to 3 times.

INHALE AND EXHALE

Standing normally, take one step forward, opening your arms and breathing deeply. Hold your breath for a few seconds, then exhale while stepping back. Repeat 3 to 5 times for relaxation.

STRENGTH TRAINING

Another form of exercise that many modern judoka use is strength training. Although judo is the art of using an opponent's strength against him or her, it is a mistake to think that one's personal strength is not important. The goal of martial-arts training has always been to maximize personal development.

Before undergoing a weight-training program specific to judo, one must follow a general conditioning program that targets the legs, chest, shoulders, back, arms, abdomen, and lower back. To avoid creating muscular imbalance, it is important to work opposing pairs of muscle groups equally—quadriceps and hamstrings, chest and upper back, biceps and triceps, abdomen and lower back. A basic, all-around program might include squats and dead lifts for the legs, bench press for the chest, bent rows for the back, sit-ups for the abdomen, and good mornings for the lower back. One should pay special attention to the abdominal muscles, the foundation of the human body for health and fitness. The abdominal muscles are crucial to the generation of strength and power because they connect the upper and lower body.

Weight training is typically done according to this formula: number of sets × number of reps × weight. To start, 3 sets of 10 reps of each exercise with a weight that one can comfortably lift 10 times will accomplish the goal of general conditioning. The novice weightlifter should follow this program for a minimum of two to three months before beginning any judo-specific training.

When weight training, the judoka should apply martial-arts breathing to the movements, exhaling during the application of power and breathing in deeply from the abdomen when inhaling to prepare for the next application of strength.

The serious judoka who wishes to increase muscular strength, power, and explosiveness should incorporate a more complex set of exercises. For this regimen, the poundage should be high and the number of sets and repetitions low. Before beginning any such program, the judoka should consult someone experienced in the following lifts to learn proper technique. Failure to do so will limit the effectiveness of the exercises and may result in injury. Some useful exercises for judo include power cleans, snatch, push press, push jerk, squats, high pulls, bench, pull-ups, plyometric drills, and medicine-ball trunk throws. Of course, one would not do all these exercises on the same day. A typical day might include power cleans, squats, push press, good mornings, and trunk throws. Combinations of the exercises can also be implemented, such as clean and jerk or squat and push press. The judoka should perform 3 to 5 sets of 6 reps for each exercise with a rest of one and a half to two minutes between sets. The focus should be on explosion, that is, moving the weight as fast as possible with control. One should do that type of weight training no more than twice per week.

If the aim of the program is muscular endurance, circuit training is an excellent option. Circuit training involves following one exercise immediately with another, with no rest between exercises, until one completes the entire circuit. A typical circuit designed for judo would consist of 8 to 10 exercises and take between five and seven minutes to complete (coincidentally the length of a judo match). Doing three circuits with a rest period of five minutes following each circuit is ideal. To gain the cardiovascular benefit of circuits, one should do circuit training at least twice per week.

Remember that even prodigious gains in strength and endurance do not translate directly into better judo ability. Weight training is only a supplement to judo training. The best way to improve at judo is by doing judo.

ENDURANCE TRAINING

Weight training is just one of the methods that a judoka can use to improve physical condition. Many judoka add running to their exercise program. Running builds aerobic capacity, which gives the judo practitioner extra endurance for tournament play. To maintain the pace required for a judo shiai, the judoka must have endurance. One who has never practiced randori or participated in a shiai cannot begin to imagine the expenditure of energy necessary to compete.

The type of running a judoka should do depends on his or her level of competition and phase of training. Remember that all off-mat training should be specific to judo. The novice judoka who would like to practice judo recreationally or the skilled judoka who is in the off-season should run for general conditioning. The program should consist of running at low to moderate intensity for three to five miles about three times per week. This routine will provide a good base of conditioning that will allow the judoka to train longer and harder before fatiguing.

Once general, or base, conditioning is achieved, a judoka who wishes to improve conditioning to the next level should start shortening the distance of the runs and increasing the intensity. For judo, a distance of two miles is ideal. By timing the runs, the judoka can continue to improve fitness by attempting to beat the time of the previous run. Again, the judoka should run three or four times per week with a rest day following a running day.

A more serious judoka or one who is in season competitively may want to include sprinting to improve cardiovascular performance and increase the speed and explosiveness necessary for competition. One should introduce sprinting gradually into the training program. The sprinting program should correspond to the upcoming competition. As the competition nears, the sprinting distance should become shorter and more intense. Generally, one should sprint no more than twice per week. The rest period should be twice as long as the work period (rest = 2 × sprint time). A sample running program follows.

Off-season: Run three to five miles three times per week for general or base conditioning

Preseason: Run timed two-mile runs three times per week

In-season: Perform sprints twice per week and timed two-mile runs twice per week

Sprinting (sample):

800-meter warm-up

400 meters × 4 sets, 2:1 rest-to-work ratio

800-meter cool-down

As the competition nears, the sprint distances should decrease and intensity should increase, using the same rest-to-work ratio (2:1).

400-meter warm-up

200 meters × 4 sets, 2:1 rest-to-work ratio

100 meters × 6 sets, 2:1 rest-to-work ratio

400-meter cool-down

PREPARING FOR COMPETITION

Judo competitions take place almost every weekend, but only a few major events are held each year. The type of training one employs is determined by personal goals and what phase of training the person is in. This section discusses how to prepare for a special event by using a seasonal plan. Keep in mind that judo training for the elite competitor is different from the training suitable for a recreational judoka. But the person who has decided to compete must be prepared. A few basic concepts will help the person achieve his or her goal.

Training includes four phases: off-season, preseason, in-season, and peak season. The goal of training is to be physically, mentally, and technically ready for the goal event. First, the individual must decide what event he or she wants to win and how much time is available to prepare. The person can then start to devise a training program.

The off-season phase of training begins four to six months before the competition. During this period, one should work on general conditioning, building muscle strength, developing new techniques, and refining existing ones. In judo practice, the judoka develops new techniques and refines old ones by doing uchikomi (fit-ins) and sets of throws on a crash pad. Over time, the person slowly increases the amount of randori done in each session to improve conditioning. The judoka who supplements judo training with weight training and running should focus on basic strength exercises, doing 3 sets of 8 to 10 repetitions for each major body part and running 3 miles 3 times per week.

The second phase, preseason training, starts about four months before the competition and lasts approximately 8 to 10 weeks. In this training phase, the goal is to undergo a tear-down process and develop muscle stamina. During judo practice the judoka should continue to refine techniques but should place more emphasis on randori. A minimum of 30 minutes of standing randori (6 rounds × 5 minutes) and 20 minutes of ne waza randori (5 rounds × 4 minutes) should be done with minimal rest between rounds. In the weight room, the judoka starts circuit training (going from one exercise to another without rest) to improve muscle endurance.

Running during this phase should consist of timed two-mile runs three times per week. The judoka should try to beat the time of the previous run in each outing to improve conditioning.

The in-season phase begins 6 to 8 weeks before the event. All training should be intense, focused, and geared for competition. During this period, the volume (amount of time) of training decreases and the intensity of the workouts increases. In judo practice, the judoka should do randori no more than four to six rounds (with a five-minute rest between rounds), but the rounds should be quality rounds done under competitive conditions. Another successful method of randori training for both tachi waza and ne waza is to take a lineup of 6 to 10 opponents consecutively for a minute each (or first ippon) without rest. This grueling regimen, suitable only for the serious competitor, will pay off in the end. At the end of practice, one can refine techniques by doing nagekomi (throws). Weight training should consist of an 8- to 10-station total-body circuit with no rest between stations. Each circuit should take approximately six to eight minutes to perform. The judoka does the circuit three times, resting for five minutes after each circuit. Sprinting (400 meters $\times$ 4-6) should be incorporated into the running regimen twice per week.

Peak season is the last few weeks before the event. Workouts should gradually become shorter but more intense. Tapering off about a week before the competition allows the body to heal and rest. In the last week the judoka keeps randori training to a minimum and works on timing and speed. Lifting ends altogether. The judoka should focus on the goal and think positive! He or she should start visualizing success in the event by seeing himself or herself beating the opponents. A few good nights of sleep, a healthy diet, and adequate hydration are important.

The judoka should relax the day before competition. He or she should do nothing physical, continue to eat well, drink lots of water, and get to bed early. Eating a well-balanced meal on the morning of competition is important. The contestant must make sure to maintain fluid and energy levels throughout the day of competition. Most important, the judoka must relax, be confident, know that he or she is prepared, and make it happen.

Whether you are a novice judoka who plans to practice the sport recreationally or a skilled judo competitor, it is essential that you develop your body properly. Never forget that judo itself develops the human body. Although warm-up exercises, cool-down exercises, running, and weight training are valuable, the most important aspect of judo training is judo training itself. The goal of all other training is to make your judo better, and the best way to improve your judo is to practice your judo techniques. Always warm up properly and cool down appropriately but devote the lion's share of your training time to practicing the art itself.

One of the most important "secrets" of ancient martial-arts training is that physical condition improves gradually over time. What this means is that moderate, daily training is more important than extreme, erratic training. The best way to build up your body in all facets—flexibility, strength, and endurance—is through moderate, daily training interspersed with a few intense workouts throughout the week.

SUGGESTED READINGS

Ishikawa, Takahiko, and Donn F. Draeger. 1961. *Judo Training Methods*. Rutland, Vermont: Charles E. Tuttle.

Kano, Jigoro. 1986. *Kodokan Judo*. Tokyo: Kodansha International, Ltd.

Kudo, Kazuzo. 1966. *Dynamic Judo* (two volumes). Tokyo: Japan Publications Trading Company.

Nishioka, Hayward, and James R. West. 1979. *The Judo Textbook*. Burbank, California: Ohara.

Takagaki, Shinzo, and Harold E. Sharp. 1957. *The Techniques of Judo*. Rutland, Vermont: Charles E. Tuttle.

Tamura, Vince, and Gene Shelton. 1974. *Common Sense Self Defense*. Burbank, California: Ohara.

Watanabe, Jiichi, and Lindy Avakian. 1960. *The Secrets of Judo*. Rutland, Vermont: Charles E. Tuttle.

INDEX

ABOUT THE AUTHORS

Jimmy Pedro has been the top-ranked American judoka for the past decade. He has won national titles five times. Pedro is also the world champion in the 73-kg (161-lb.) category. Pedro is a three-time Olympian and 1996 Olympic bronze medallist. Pedro holds a fifth-degree black belt and has practiced judo for 25 years with his father and longtime coach, Jim Pedro, Sr.

Pedro resides in Lawrence, Massachusetts, with his wife, Marie, and their three children.

Writer William Durbin, an accomplished student and practitioner of martial arts with a third-degree black belt in judo, assisted Pedro in the development of the book. Durbin is considered one of the world's foremost authorities and historians on martial arts. Among his numerous martial arts honors are Presidential Sports Awards for karate and judo. Durbin and his wife, Carol, reside in Frankfort, Kentucky.